Good Practice Guide: **Keeping Out of Trouble**

Good Practice Guide:
Keeping Out of Trouble

Owen Luder CBE
Past President Royal Institute of British Architects
Past Chairman of the Architects Registration Board

RIBA Publishing

© Owen Luder, 2012, on behalf of Keeping Out of Trouble Ltd
Published by RIBA Publishing, 15 Bonhill Street, London EC2P 2EA

First published 1999. Second edition 2002. Third edition 2006. Fourth edition 2012

ISBN 978 1 85946 460 1

Stock code 77935

British Library Cataloguing-in-Publications Data
A catalogue record for this book is available from the British Library.

Commissioning Editor: James Thompson
Project Editor: Neil O'Regan
Editor: Alasdair Deas
Designed and typeset by Ben Millbank
Printed and bound by MPG Books, Cornwall

RIBA Publishing is part of RIBA Enterprises Ltd.

www.ribaenterprises.com

Dedication

This guide is dedicated to all those who helped to keep me out of trouble during my time as a practising architect and to all those young architects just starting their careers in this wonderful profession. I hope it will help them avoid those practice tripwires and keep them out of trouble.

Series foreword

The *Good Practice Guide* series has been specifically developed to provide architects, and other construction professionals, with practical advice and guidance on a range of topics which affect them, and the management of their business, on a day-to-day basis.

All of the guides in the series are written in an easy-to-read, straightforward style. The guides are not meant to be definitive texts on the particular subject in question, but each guide will be the reader's first point of reference, offering them a quick overview of the key points and then provide them with a 'route map' for finding further, more detailed information. Where appropriate, checklists, tables, diagrams and case studies will be included to aid ease-of-use.

Good Practice Guide: Keeping Out of Trouble

That this RIBA Good Practice Guide is now in its fourth edition, and remains a much-used bestseller 14 years after its first appearance in 1999, demonstrates its continued usefulness to architects and students. It covers 'where things go wrong' – a distillation of Owen Luder's 50 years in architectural practice, as an expert witness, as a mediator, and on the ARB's Investigation and Disciplinary committees. It is not a practice manual in itself, but a valuable aide-memoire to refer to when dealing with clients and fees, contracts, the law, the ARB and the RIBA – identifying in each case the tripwires you need to avoid if you are to keep out of trouble.

Angela Brady
President, RIBA

Preface

In the introduction to the first edition of this guide in 1999 I wrote:

Practising architecture is a fascinating, creative occupation that offers far more than just earning a living. The excitement of landing that wonderful new project to design is only matched by the feeling of achievement of walking round the finished building that you have created from a blank sheet of paper.

This has not changed. But the world in which we practise is constantly changing.

When I first started a practice, architecture was a relatively low risk profession with a more relaxed competition for work. Mandatory fees meant little if any negotiation over fees, and there were far fewer legal and practical tripwires to get the unwary young architect into trouble than there are today.

Court cases were rare, with problems resolved around the table without the help of lawyers. Today, disputes and potential legal claims are always just around the corner.

Fees are now very competitive. Competition for work with other architects, as well as with other organisations offering architectural services, is fierce. Many more people not directly involved in the building contract now have a legal right to claim against the architect if they consider they have suffered damage as a result of something we have done or should have done.

New laws and the application of existing laws are continuously increasing our responsibilities and legal liabilities. The increased complexity of building design and construction and the number of other people now involved have increased the possibilities for errors and misunderstandings.

The potential for getting into trouble with clients, fees, building contracts and with the law is huge. The tripwires for the unwary are everywhere.

This guide highlights the many areas where problems are likely to arise, how to recognise them and then avoid them, and if that is not possible at least how to minimise the most adverse effects on you and your practice.

This edition, as before, is not intended to be, nor could it be, a comprehensive architectural practice manual. It covers what, in my experience, are the most common areas where things go wrong and will get you into trouble. Some of the tripwires identified are obvious, and yet architects and others still keep falling over them, sometimes with serious consequences..

While the book aims to avoid quoting practice, contract or other documents which can become dated, where such documents are quoted, make sure you check they are still up to date and whether any practice notes have been published that relate to them.

Understanding and avoiding the tripwires identified in this guide should enable you to enjoy a more profitable and satisfying practice in what is still, despite all the changes, the most exciting, challenging, creative and satisfying profession.

Owen Luder CBE PPRIBA FRSA MAE
May 2012

About the author

Owen Luder CBE PPRIBA FRSA MAE was uniquely twice elected RIBA President (1981–83 and 1995–97) and Vice Chairman and Chairman of the Architects Registration Board (1997–2003) and was a nationally elected member of the RIBA Council almost continuously from 1967 to 1998. He was elected again to the RIBA Council in 2010 and so is still involved actively in architectural practice and the governance of the profession.

He qualified in 1954 and started his own 'one-man' office in the late 1950s, which grew into a major architectural practice with offices in Wales, Harrogate and Newcastle in the UK and associated offices in Nigeria and Saudi Arabia. He was responsible for the design and construction of many large commercial, industrial, retail, leisure and housing projects, urban and environmental planning and regeneration schemes in the UK and abroad.

In 1976 his practice, the Owen Luder Partnership, converted to company status. In 1987 he withdrew to revert to being a one-man band, working as an independent architect, urban designer and marketing and construction consultant. He is a member of the Academy of Experts and a qualified mediator.

From 1984 to 1991 he organised, chaired and was a speaker for the RIBA Services Practice seminars, and from then until 2003 organised the Building Design practice update seminars. He still lectures to Part 3 students and young architects on 'Keeping Out of Trouble'.

He was editor and presenter for the *Architectural Practice* videos and a regular columnist for many years with *Building* and *Building Design* magazines. He was awarded the publishers' Business Columnist of the Year award in 1987.

Keeping Out of Trouble is a distillation of his over 50 years of experience in architectural practice and construction, combining what he describes as his own mistakes learned the hard way and the mistakes of others he has seen, commented on as an expert witness or helped to resolve as a mediator.

Acknowledgements

I would like to thank all those people who have helped to keep me out of trouble in writing the latest edition of this guide – in particular Adam Williamson of the RIBA, Simon Howard of the Architects Registration Board, and Koko Udom for advice on contracts and legal issues.

In the original editions I would like to thank in particular Bill Gloyn, the Chairman of the Commercial Property Practice Group at AON Ltd, Richard Coleman, the Assistant Registrar at the Architects Registration Board, and Richard Brindley and Jane Muir of the Practice Department of the RIBA.

Finally, my wife, Jacqui, who gave me positive and helpful advice on format and content as the writing progressed. Sadly she died in 2008, but she would be delighted that the book that she first helped create in its previous editions warrants a further edition after 15 years and is still helping students and architects to 'Keep Out of Trouble'.

Contents

Section 1
Keeping out of trouble with clients

Clients come in three sizes: great clients, good clients, clients from hell!

Clients are the most important people in the design and construction process. Without clients there are no buildings to design. Without clients, who will pay the fees that pay your bills? And remember, clients are difficult to win, but very easy to lose.

You are more likely to be involved in a legal dispute with a client than with anyone else in the construction process. Clients can claim damages against you for alleged professional negligence. They can refuse to pay your fees. They can complain about you to the Architects Registration Board and the Royal Institute of British Architects.

Rather than accepting work from a client from hell, you may be wiser to send a cheque for £10,000 to an architect you least like and get them to do the job. It will cost you less that way!

So – know your clients

You need new work continually. A large proportion of this should come from your existing clients. So look after them at all times. But you also need new clients. They are a great opportunity to design an exciting building, make your name and expand your practice and your profits!

But clients come in all shapes and sizes:

- The great client, who you would give your right arm to work for.
- The good client, who knows what they want and are prepared to pay the proper fee for it – providing you deliver the service you promised.
- The 'client from hell', who will cost you time, money and unending anguish if you get involved with them. To be avoided like the plague!

So do check out new clients carefully before you decide to work with them. Identify those you may have difficulty working with and will lose money on, however well you perform. Then decide whether you can afford to risk working for them!

Problems with clients often stem from the fact that clients and the architect are incompatible. Will you get on with each other? Your relationship with your client is vital to the success of the project. Can you work with them and can they work with you? Are you on the same wavelength architecturally? If not, is it worth risking embarking on a relationship that is likely to end in tears – or even worse?

Check out a new client before you get too deeply involved

Check with people who are working with, or have worked with, your prospective new client. You will be surprised at the number of people you know, either directly or indirectly, who can help you. Ask them what they know about your new client, and particularly if they know how the client deals with the people with whom they have business relationships.

A telephone call is usually better than a letter as people are often nervous about putting adverse comments on paper – they will be more open in their comments in an 'off the record' chat.

So, find out how they are organised. Do they listen, make objective decisions and remain consistent in their decisions? Are they efficient? Can they be trusted? Do they pay on time?

If you receive negative signals from these questions, think hard before making a commitment to work with them. If you do decide to proceed, take these negative signals into account when you negotiate your fees. The more potentially difficult the client, the bigger the risk you are taking in working for them and the higher the fee you will need to cover that increased risk.

Reconnaissance always pays off!

Who is your client?

Claims for fees can fail, or fees can be very difficult to recover, if you are chasing payment with the wrong person or company.

Clients are not always what they appear to be at the outset. Be quite clear, and if in doubt establish the legal identity of your client. Who will sign your fee cheques?

Who will you name in the legal claim form (writ) if you have to sue for non-payment of fees?

If the client is a company, who will sign your fee agreement and your fee cheques?

If your client is one of a group of companies, then which company? If a subsidiary company, is it a £100 shell company with no assets? If so, you require a guarantee from the parent company that your fees will be paid.

Who will be responsible for paying your fees? Check that the company or person with whom you negotiated your fee agreement is actually the one who signs it. Also, is this the person who will subsequently instruct you to go ahead with the project and who will sign the building contract?

"Time spent clarifying who your client is, who will pay your fees and who has authority to give you instructions should avoid serious problems later, which otherwise would cost you in time and money."

If there is a change of client identity at any stage, challenge it, and do not agree to the change unless you are satisfied your financial and legal positions have not been weakened. Would you have agreed to work for the 'new' client at the agreed fees at the outset?

If the individuals or company who negotiated and signed your fee agreement cease to exist – the company has been put into liquidation, or your married couple clients have divorced – before proceeding any further you must sort out who will continue as your client and who will pay your fees!

Apart from fees, establish and confirm in writing who is authorised to give you instructions. Only accept instructions from that person or their authorised representatives. If it is a company, which executive has that responsibility? If your client is a married couple or partners, which one gives the instructions? Divorce proceedings have been known to follow from confusion over this issue between husband and wife, as well as an expensive dispute with their architect!

Time spent clarifying who your client is, who will pay your fees and who has authority to give you instructions should avoid serious problems later, which otherwise would cost you in time and money.

Can they – will they – pay you?

If you do not get paid, you have wasted your time!

Whether your client is an individual or a company, check they have the financial resources to carry out the project and pay your fees before you become too deeply committed. The bigger the project and the fees involved, the more important this is. Small jobs that go wrong can give you a headache. Big jobs can bankrupt you!

Your bank and accountant should be able to help. Who else is working for your client? Who do you know who does business with them who can give you 'off the record' comments?

If you are dealing with a company, Companies House in Cardiff will send you annual accounts, the names of the directors and other basic information. If it is a publicly quoted company, contact the head office and ask for a copy of their last three years' published accounts. Watch the financial pages for any adverse news about that company. Monitor their website and share price. Time spent checking is invariably time well spent.

It should not embarrass your potential client that you are checking them out! If they are a commercial organisation it will be part of their normal business to check the financial credentials of people or companies with whom they deal and give credit. Remember, because your service is provided in advance of being paid, you are continually at risk and are in effect giving credit to your client.

If your client does change identity (from an individual to a company, for example), check your new client is as financially sound as the original. If necessary, ask your original client for appropriate guarantees before agreeing to the change. Negotiate up-front fees to reduce your exposure if you have serious doubts about their creditability.

If the building project on which you are working is sold and you are passed on as the architect with the site, check that the new client is as financially stable as the original! Your new client may be one of those with whom you cannot afford to work, or who will warrant a higher fee to cover an increased risk.

Be tough if you have any doubts about the changed client, particularly if they need you more than you need them. If you can, negotiate a higher fee to cover the increased risk, particularly as the changeover will probably involve you in some additional work.

Experience shows that recurring sources of problems in modern practice are when sites and buildings on which architects have been working are sold on to other developers, or when design–build contractors are appointed to carry on with developments using the architects' designs and drawings. These events can lead to copyright and novation issues, which are dealt with in later sections. The safest way to deal with such situations is to anticipate them and negotiate a covering clause in your fee agreement.

Try at all times when negotiating or dealing with problems to be in the postion where your client needs you more than you need them!

Do not allow a change of client identity to go unchallenged.

Periodically monitor the financial position of clients

While large projects earn big fees and a long-term workload, it is best to maintain a variety of different sized projects in the practice. This is far safer – a single enormous project may be exciting, but if it goes badly wrong it may destroy you financially.

Also, keep track of the financial strength of your clients during progress of projects. A client who is financially sound at the outset may get into financial trouble later. At the first signs of potential problems (late payment of accounts is often an early indication), reduce your financial exposure to them as quickly as you can. *Do not allow it to increase!*

'Blue-chip' clients can go bust, creating the collapsing 'pack of cards' effect. Rolls Royce in the 1970s and the Robert Maxwell saga and Enron collapse are examples of large public companies that go bust and drag down many smaller companies and individuals with them.

Keep a check on the value of your work in progress and unpaid fees with any one client. You cannot afford to be overexposed on any one job or with any single client. When negotiating fees for very big projects, build in regular staged fee payments to safeguard against getting too exposed. Staged payment is now a statutory requirement for all construction contracts with contract works of a duration of 45 days or more under the Housing Grants, Construction and Regeneration Act 1996 as amended by the Local Democracy, Economic Development and Construction Act

2009 (Construction Act as amended). If outstanding fees build up alarmingly, consider stopping work until you are paid all your outstanding fees. If necessary, refuse to restart until the outstanding fees are paid. If you are still concerned, insist on payments of further fees in advance. If you decide to stop work, it is important to follow the procedure set out in your contract. The Construction Act as amended provides for seven days' notice before suspension. The Act also allows you to suspend some or all of your duties under a construction contract on account of outstanding debt by a client and entitles you to payment of reasonable costs and expenses arising as a result of such suspension (architectural, design and surveying work fall within the ambit of construction contracts as defined by the Construction Act).

If your client gets into financial trouble and goes into liquidation, that will create cash-flow problems for you and may take you into bankruptcy with them.

Avoid at all times becoming overexposed to outstanding fees or unpaid work completed for any one client – or on any single project.

Novation

Problems also arise when the client for whom you have designed the building hands over the detail design and construction to a design–build contractor, with you as the novated architect.

"If you are being novated, make sure you are comfortable with the terms of your new appointment."

In those circumstances, your client is now the design–builder, not your original client. Your role and responsibilities will have been changed! Invariably, when the client changes, for whatever reason, the requirements and objectives of the new client will be different, and so too will your responsibilities.

So, ensure you agree any changes to the brief; clarify your changed role and responsibilities with both parties and agree any additional fees before you commit yourself to continuing. Later will be too late!

Make sure any novation agreement including the fees to be paid between original client and design–build contractor is agreed by you and signed by all three parties before you start work for the design–build contractor.

If you are being novated, make sure you are comfortable with the terms of your new appointment.

'Communication' is listening as much as speaking

Many problems stem from a lack of communication between architects and clients. People, sometimes architects (and often politicians), talk well but do not listen.

You may have already designed a new award-winning house in your mind. You only want to hear what the client says if it fits with your preconceived conception of what you think they ought to have rather than what they actually want! If you impose on your client what you think they should have, rather than what they need, it will come back and bite you later!

So, when discussing projects with your clients, are you really listening? Do you understand what is being said? Do you want to understand? Can you hear what your clients are telling you about their needs?

Nelson put his telescope to his blind eye when he did not want to carry out the instruction he was being given. He died a hero. You are unlikely to be so lucky!

Oral instructions are difficult to prove!

If it is not in writing, it is your word against theirs.

If you finish up in court, the judge will decide the dispute on the factual evidence before them. If there is conflicting oral evidence, the judge is more likely to give the benefit of the doubt to the lay client: it was up to you as the professional to have ensured the uncertainty did not arise.

If, for example, you need to take short cuts to start work on site to achieve the client's timetable, or need to reduce design and specification standards to meet their budget costs, ensure they understand and agree to the risks and extra costs that may be involved. Later, when the contract is in trouble because of these changes, it will be too late to tell them it was their fault because they did not give you sufficient time to do your job properly. Or that the roof leaks because you had to cut the cost to meet their budget!

At all times, make sure you have clear instructions and make notes of decisions agreed orally with your clients when they are being agreed. If those instructions are changed, or cannot be carried out as originally envisaged, discuss and agree these further changes with them. Read back what you have noted as agreed to avoid later misunderstandings or arguments. *Then confirm in writing without delay!*

If necessary send the confirmation by fax or e-mail as well as by post. If you have doubts about the integrity of the client, send a copy of the e-mail to yourself at the same time so that you can, if necessary, prove that it was sent and had been received.

If your client wishes to change the design or work, be certain that you and they fully understand the implications of the changes they have requested. Will they trigger a contractor's claim for delay and disruption? How much extra cost and/or delay will be involved? Will they affect the work of other consultants? Will you be entitled to extra fees? If so, find out how much is involved and report this to your client. Identify whether these changes mean more work for you and whether you are justified in asking for additional fees.

If so, get agreement to your extra costs or fees before you have carried out the work. Do not wait until the end of the contract to ask for more fees. At best you will have an argument with your client; at worst you will not get paid.

Confirm what has been agreed in writing to your clients and the consultants involved without delay!

Do be careful if you are asked to pass on client's instructions to other consultants appointed direct by the client. Avoid risking becoming involved in fee disputes that arise from client changes that result in extra work for those consultants.

The JCT standard contract forms and the RIBA standard forms of appointment provide for client changes and for the cost to be priced and agreed before execution. Be disciplined and ensure these arrangements are complied with. The client then knows the cost before they are committed and can change their mind again if they do not like the extra cost.

You must avoid the situation where the client can say: 'If I had known that it would cost that amount extra, and would delay completion, I would not have agreed to the change'. If they can legitimately say this, you will have a problem.

If that is not possible, ensure that the client is aware that they have asked for changes that will cost extra money, and that they wish the changes to be made before the extra cost can be established. In any event, when established confirm to them the extra cost *in writing* without delay.

If changes are necessary because problems have arisen with the design or construction that are significant and will involve delay or additional costs, you must advise your client of the nature of the problem, the options available to them and, if you have a recommendation, which option you advise should be followed and why. Then leave the client to decide which option they wish to follow and to instruct you accordingly. *Confirm in writing immediately.*

Do not take on responsibility for making decisions that should be made by the client. You will get no thanks from them if you are right, and possibly a writ for negligence if you are wrong!

Dealing with clients' complaints

Small scratches become big sores and then go septic if not attended to quickly!

If not dealt with quickly and effectively, minor complaints by clients (and others) can fester and rapidly grow into major problems, and then into costly disputes. They slow down fee payments, and may eventually lead to allegations of negligence! Monitor continuously all work in your office for problems and deal with them before they become a major issue or – even worse – a disaster!

Keep an eye on all your ongoing work. Have a regular agenda item at partners' or directors' board meetings where whoever is chairing the meeting asks everyone present the direct question: 'Are you aware of any problems on any projects or with office matters that have not previously been reported and discussed?'

Press the point. Watch for body language. Whoever is responsible may be too embarrassed to own up, but they must to avoid the risk of bigger trouble later on.

If you are a sole practitioner, set aside a specific time every week or every month to review all your jobs and check if there are any problems, known or arising, and then deal with them immediately. *Problems rarely solve themselves.*

Put in place a formal procedure for handling clients' complaints so they are dealt with rapidly and efficiently. This should, in most cases, prevent relatively minor items drifting into becoming major problems that may lead to loss of goodwill with your clients and unpaid fees. Having set up a system, monitor it regularly to ensure it is being operated properly throughout your office.

A properly organised complaints procedure will also ensure prompt discussion with your clients, enabling you to take speedy and positive action to deal with the complaint and so minimise its impact on the project, on your fee payments and on client goodwill.

The procedure will also give you advance warning of any potential negligence claim situations of which you need to notify your professional indemnity insurance (PII) provider. Section 6 describes the risks of non-notification of matters that may lead to a claim against your PII policy.

See also:
Notifications
of potential
claims to insur-
ers, page 122

Follow the procedures set out in the *Architects Code*, the Architects Registration Board (ARB)'s code of conduct and practice. RIBA members must also follow the principles in the RIBA *Code of Professional Conduct*, and in particular the advice in Code Guidance Note 9 on complaints and dispute resolution. They are no more than good practice and will help to keep you out of trouble, not only with the ARB and the RIBA but also with your clients. They will also help you avoid submitting a fee account when your client has a complaint about your work, you or your staff, which will almost certainly delay payment until the problem is resolved.

See also: The
Architects
Code, page 130,
and
RIBA Code of
Professional
Conduct,
page 138

Adjoining owners' rights

Neighbour disputes are increasing and can be vitriolic and costly! Costly to you if they arise from something you have not, or should not have, done in your work for your client.

Problems can arise when adjoining owners' rights or concerns are not recognised early enough. Not taking the required action early can result in delays and extra costs.

Assess as early as possible the implications of all adjoining owners' property rights and also where the owners may have justifiable concerns about what is proposed. Establish what must be agreed with them and what ought to be discussed out of courtesy, if only to encourage good neighbourly relations and to avoid problems later. Agree whether your client will make informal contact with adjoining owners to explain to them what is proposed or whether you as the architect should make formal approaches.

Get the adjoining owners on side early on. Your client is likely to have to make fewer concessions at that stage. Later on, people's views become increasingly entrenched. The deeper each side digs in, the more difficult it is to get them to agree!

In urban areas, local residents' views will be important for planning applications. Assess possible local objections. Discuss these with your clients and agree a strategy to head off opposition. Time taken to get residents and amenity associations on your side will be time well spent. Do not wait for them to become objectors.

Neighbours from hell can be nearly as bad as clients from hell!

Party walls

Party wall notices apply in all parts of the country. You cannot start work on or near party walls until the necessary notices have been served and the time limits required by law have expired or an agreement has been reached with the adjoining owner.

Remember that party wall notices may have to be served if the work proposed is within a prescribed distance of your client's boundary, even without a party wall. Ensure your client understands the need for the party wall notice and agrees the work involved, and that they are responsible for the adjoining owner's surveyor's fees as well as yours.

Discuss informally with the adjoining owner the work that your client has in mind and how this will be carried out. Explain (if they are not aware) their right to a formal notice and appoint a surveyor to agree to the work involved. Get as much as possible agreed before the party wall notice is served.

If you have overlooked serving the party wall notice and this causes a delay, particularly after building has commenced, at best you will have a disgruntled client; at worst you could have a negligence claim.

Do not risk starting any work covered by the party wall regulations until the notice has been served and the necessary procedures completed.

Building start date

Make sure that in your client's programme the time allocated for you to design and to start building is realistic and allows you the time to do your job properly.

Tell them what they should know, rather than what they want to hear, on start and completion dates. If there are delays in agreeing the design or obtaining planning consent, get them to agree to move the start date as necessary.

Ensure you have served the necessary statutory notices and dealt with any planning approval conditions and any other matters that have to be complied with before work can start on site before you allow the client to sign a building contract that commits the contractor to starting on site by a contract date.

"Make sure that in your client's programme the time allocated for you to design and to start building is realistic and allows you the time to do your job properly."

If you allow a situation to be created where the contractor can claim for a delayed start, your client will almost certainly hold you responsible! Even if not serious enough for a negligence claim, they may withhold payment of your fees as compensation!

Do not agree to a start date on site until you are satisfied that it can be achieved.

Do you fully understand the building contract you are asking your client to sign?

It is vital that you and your project architect are fully conversant with the duties the building contract to be signed by the client places on you as the architect.

You must keep fully up to date with the revisions to standard contract forms as they are issued. Track the law case and practice reports that appear regularly in the technical press which highlight problems that have arisen in practice.

Be fully conversant with the current suite of JCT standard contract forms and all other contract forms in use in construction. Make sure you are up to date with all updates, amendments and advisory notes. If your client wishes to use one of the other contract forms available, ensure you fully understand their requirements and your duties where they differ from the standard JCT contract forms. Ideally use standard forms that you use generally and avoid 'ad hoc' contract forms.

You cannot afford not to be completely up to date at all times with the building contracts used on your projects.

Does your client understand the building contract to be signed?

Client problems often arise because they do not understand the obligations they enter into, and why, when they sign a building contract.

Few lay clients are likely to understand the full implications of the contract you are asking them to sign. So, take time to explain to them why you have suggested that contract form and ensure they are fully aware of the obligations they take on before they sign. This is particularly important for domestic or 'consumer' clients who have the added protection of consumer law, which makes it incumbent upon you, the expert consultant, to ensure that any contract conditions are fully explained and are understood by a 'non-expert consumer' client.

Make sure that your client understands the following:

- They must give possession of the whole of the site on the dates specified in the contract. They must understand that failure to do so will result in a claim from the contractor, which may have serious financial consequences for them.
- They must pay the architect's certificates on time. Not to do so will not only create bad relations with the contractor but could also lead to the contractor terminating the contract, with serious potential financial damages to the client.
- Your duty as contract administrator is to act impartially between clients and contractors in certain areas of the contract. Many clients find it difficult to understand that although they are paying the architect's fees, the architect must follow the terms of the contract and act impartially between them and the contractor in certain circumstances. If this explanation is left until there are problems and you make decisions that appear to favour the contractor, your client may question why, when they are paying your fees, you are making decisions against them.
- They must not give instructions directly to contractors or sub-contractors. The client must understand that direct instructions bypassing the architect will inevitably lead to confusion, delays and extra costs – which they will have to pay.
- Making changes while the work is under way will almost certainly result in extra costs, and perhaps delays – so no changes unless they are unavoidable. This applies to the architect as well!

Ensure that it is clearly defined and agreed who in a client organisation, or within married couples or partnerships, has the authority to give you instructions for changes under the contract. Make sure your client is aware who, on your side, is in charge of the administration of the contract and has your authority to accept instructions. JCT contracts include the appointment of the architect who will be the 'contract administrator'. Ensure clients are aware of this and try where possible to funnel all important contract issues through the contract administrator. Avoid a host of people on the client's side and on yours from all giving and receiving instructions.

Problems will almost certainly arise if clients decide to appoint specialist sub-contractors, outside the main building contract which is under your control, such as the appointment of specialist kitchen contractors in a domestic project.

You must ensure everyone is clear as to whether they are under your control as contract administrator, and if not then who gives them instructions and how will they liaise with you and your contractors. If they are on site at the same time as the main contractor warn your client of the complications and almost inevitable problems that will arise.

> - If clients request changes, make sure the cost and time implications are made clear to them at the time and are not left to be sorted out later. Confirm the advice you give them in writing.
> - Keep clients informed of any major issues or problems that arise on site during the contract, particularly time or cost overruns. You may consider a minor design change not worth bothering them with, but it may be of great importance to them! Avoid giving them unpleasant surprises later.

Sophisticated clients will most likely select the contract form to be used and tell you what they want covered in the contract documents. But watch for amendments they wish to make to the standard contract form and ensure you are clear how those amendments change your role and responsibilities in the administration of the contract.

Where you are asked to administer the contract on a contract form that you do not usually use, make sure you fully understand all its differing requirements and that others working on the project understand the differences as well.

If you have any concerns with the contract form the client has selected, or that any changes they wish to make may lead to problems, you must set out those concerns to your client so that they are aware and accept the risks involved. This will also help to safeguard your position should problems subsequently arise in the areas you have highlighted.

If you have serious concerns and your client proceeds despite your advice, confirm your reservations in writing and if necessary decline to administer the contract.

Be aware that if problems arise and you finish up in court, a lay client could (and most likely would) successfully claim ignorance of the conditions of the contract as a defence and blame you for not warning them of the potential problems. Sophisticated 'developer' clients would be expected to be more aware, but do not rely on that to get you out of trouble – the judge may well take the view that you should have warned them and did not.

As a professional advisor you have a duty to warn even experienced clients. If they are lay clients not experienced in these matters, and possibly protected by consumer law, even more so.

Town planning applications

You cannot guarantee any planning approval will be granted: do not allow your clients to think you can!

Make clients aware early on of the non-returnable planning fees (and other statutory fees due later) that have to be paid *by them* when submitting the planning application. Also make them aware of the practice of some planning authorities to automatically refuse applications they cannot deal with within the statutory eight weeks. This can be very embarrassing to explain once it has happened.

Advise clients as early as possible of the realistic time required for obtaining the planning approval, without which work cannot start on site. Almost invariably obtaining planning consents takes longer – rarely, if ever, shorter – than anyone envisages at the outset.

Advise clients early on whether the planning authority will insist that detailed design drawings must be submitted with the planning application for it to be considered. If you have not allowed for this degree of detail in your appointment agreement discuss and agree at that stage any additional fees involved. With alterations or extensions to a listed building full design drawings will certainly be required.

With work to listed buildings explain clearly to the client at the outset the complicated and time-consuming negotiations that will probably be necessary with English Heritage and the planning officer before the design can be finalised and a listed building consent application submitted that should then be approved.

If clients want to make changes to a listed building that in your experience are unlikely to be approved, emphasise this to them early on and explain the appeal process, the costs and time delays involved, and the chances in your opinion of a refusal being overturned on appeal.

Be careful too to advise your clients that planning applications in conservation areas will be subject to higher degrees of control.

With complex applications in urban areas the planners will often require a collection of additional specialist reports and assessments in relation to your application. These can be costly and time consuming to produce. Make sure you establish what will be required early on and advise your clients of what will be required and the cost and time involved.

If, to save time, a client wants detailed design and production drawings started before planning approval has been obtained, ensure (and confirm this in writing) they understand the risks involved. The implications could be:

- significant changes to the drawings, required by the planners or as a result of conditions attached to the approval when received, or
- a complete redesign, to be submitted with a revised application, or, worst of all,
- if the application is refused, the client will have to abandon the project.

If you foresee problems with the planners and/or strong local opposition, advise the client early on of the procedures and possible cost of appeals against a refusal or imposition of unacceptable conditions. If the application raises issues of wider public importance, warn the client of the possibility of a public enquiry and the likely timescale and costs.

Never be anything other than totally realistic about the time required for obtaining the necessary planning approval and the lack of certainty in obtaining an acceptable planning approval.

Conflicts of interest

In situations where architects are acting as independent, impartial advisors to the client, any potential conflict of interest that could put the architect's impartial role into question should be avoided.

Conflicts of interest arise where an architect's activities, interests or commitments, perhaps even outside their architectural practice, may impinge, or appear to impinge, on their ability to give clear, impartial, independent advice to their client or act impartially between the client and other parties involved in the contract or their professional work.

The ARB's code of conduct and practice, *The Architects Code* (see Section 7), covers this issue under its Standard 1, which states:

See also: The Architects Code, page 130

> *You are expected at all times to act with honesty and integrity and to avoid any actions or situations which are inconsistent with your professional obligations. This standard underpins the Code and will be taken to be required in any consideration of your conduct under any of the other standards.*

Paragraph 1.3 of the ARB code's guidance notes states:

> *Where a conflict of interest arises you are expected to disclose it in writing and manage it to the satisfaction of all affected parties. You should seek written confirmation that all parties involved give their informed consent to your continuing to act. Where this consent is not received you should cease acting for one or more of the parties.*

The ARB requirement covers your responsibility to 'other relevant parties', which includes, for example, your responsibility to act impartially between clients and contractors and others involved in the building contract as well as with your clients.

The *RIBA Code of Professional Conduct* contains similar requirements under Principle 1 – Honesty and Integrity.

> 1.   *Principle 1 – Honesty and Integrity*
> 1.1 *The Royal Institute expects its Members to act with impartiality, responsibility and truthfulness at all times in their professional and business activities.*
> 1.2 *Members should not allow themselves to be improperly influenced either by their own, or others', self-interest.*
> 1.3 *Members should not be a party to any statement which they know to be untrue, misleading, unfair to others or contrary to their own professional knowledge.*
> 1.4 *Members should avoid conflicts of interest. If a conflict arises, they should declare it to those parties affected and either remove its cause, or withdraw from that situation.*

1.5   Members should respect confidentiality and the privacy of others.

1.6   Members should not offer or take bribes in connection with their professional work.

More detailed guidance and advice can be found in Guidance Note 1 (Integrity, Conflicts of Interest, Confidentiality and Privacy, Corruption and Bribery), Guidance Note 4 (Appointments) and Guidance Note 7 (Relationships).

You are the best person to identify if you are in, or drifting into, a position where a conflict of interest may affect your ability to give impartial advice to, or act impartially for, your client.

Since the removal of the ban on simultaneous practice in 1981, architects can act as developers, contractors and other occupations, which can give rise to conflicts of interest. The areas where significant problems may arise are when you are acting as developer or contractor and at the same time as the designer. You are not allowed to act as an independent advisor to the client in the design and construction of a building for which you are also the contractor. *The two roles must be kept quite separate.*

Problems often arise, particularly on smaller contracts, where at the outset of the project the architect is acting in the traditional professional advisor role. At some stage this drifts into an architect/contractor situation, which then will almost certainly create a conflict of interest situation.

It is vital that at all times both you and your client are absolutely clear as to the service you are providing to them. The best advice is to take on one role or the other; do not attempt to do both, even if you think it is helping your client to take on the role of contractor and manage the building work!

There have been several charges of unprofessional conduct to the ARB Professional Conduct Committee in which conflict of interest has been one of the complaints. The most usual situation is where an architect has recommended a contractor to carry out the building work and the client subsequently discovered that the architect had been employed by that contractor on other projects. Not an uncommon situation in modern architectural practice. In those situations, declare the relationship to the client at the outset; assure them this will not affect your handling of their project, but give them the opportunity to decline having that contractor on their tender list.

A specific example was a complaint by a client who discovered that the engineer recommended for structural design work on her extension was living with the architect. There was no real conflict of interest, but it does illustrate the care needed when recommending others for work to your clients.

Be very careful in deciding whether to accept gifts or hospitality from contractors and others with whom you have or may have business relationships. A token gift may be acceptable, but it can still be embarrassing, or even worse, when a client with whom you have a dispute finds out! To be safe only accept any form of gift or hospitality from organisations with whom you already have a working relationship where it is clearly a thank you and cannot be seen as an incentive to favour them with business opportunities.

The RIBA Code Guidance Note 1 provides some specific advice on this point:

> *An incentive to act against one's professional obligations or duty to others is a bribe. However, the exchange of small gifts and advantages in the normal course of business (such as promotional gifts or corporate hospitality) is not prohibited so long as the value to the recipient is not such that it exerts an improper influence over them.*

In all situations you must disclose any potential conflict of interest. If in doubt, remove the potential conflict of interest, and if this is not possible, withdraw from the commission.

SUMMARY

- Find out as much as you can about new clients before you get too involved.
- Are you and they compatible? If not, you may be wise not to become involved with them.
- How do they treat people with whom they conduct business?
- Are they trustworthy?
- Do they pay on time?
- Are they efficient?
- Do they have a reputation for continually changing their minds?
- Be quite clear legally who your clients are.
- Be careful of changes of identity by clients during progress.

CONTINUED ▶

SUMMARY (CONTINUED)

- If you are being novated ensure you have agreed the terms and all parties have signed the novation agreement.
- Communication is a two-way exercise – listen to what your clients are saying.
- Confirm all important discussions and oral agreements in writing.
- Do not make decisions that should be made by the clients.
- Have a system for dealing with clients' complaints – it will protect goodwill and avoid small upsets becoming major problems.
- Ensure you deal with adjoining owner issues to avoid problems.
- Do not promise what you cannot guarantee to deliver regarding planning applications.
- If you can, head off planning application objections.
- Ensure a client can give possession of the site to the contractor on the scheduled start date.
- Ensure you and your clients are fully aware of their obligations under the building contracts you will be asking them to sign.
- Identify any possible conflicts of interest and withdraw if they are unacceptable to any of the parties involved and cannot be removed.
- Clients are your most valuable assets, difficult to win and easy to lose!

Section 2
Keeping out of trouble with fees

Cash is king! If you run out of money – you go bust!

You are more likely to become involved in a legal dispute with your clients over your fees than any other issue in your practice.

A written agreement that clearly and unambiguously describes the services you are to provide and the fees you are to be paid is vital to you being paid what is properly due at the agreed time. Should you have to go to court to obtain payment without evidence of an agreement in writing, you may be at a disadvantage, even though oral contracts and agreements are now covered under the Construction Act as amended.

Fee agreements

In detail and in writing!

Many fee disputes with clients and subsequent fee recovery cases are lost or result in less being paid than properly due because no finalised fee agreement exists in writing, or where one does it does not properly cover the issues in dispute.

It is recommended that agreement on fees to be paid in return for services to be provided is confirmed in writing. This is a requirement of both the ARB and the RIBA codes of practice (see Section 7), but it is very much in your own interests, as well as your client's. Do not get sucked into doing more and more work without agreeing fees with your client to cover that work and confirming them in writing.

See also: The Architects Code, *page 130*

Without terms of appointment agreed in writing, you provide a disgruntled client (or one that just does not want to pay) with an opportunity to delay, or even avoid totally, paying you what you are otherwise properly due.

Your agreement must cover precisely *what*, *when* and *how*: what you will be paid, when you will be paid and how you will be paid. Make sure all this is spelt out clearly. Do not rely on a loose reference, such as 'as set out in the RIBA Standard Form of Appointment', or on an imprecise series of letters. If possible, use established forms of appointment (such as the RIBA's) that include fee schedules and terms for payment. If you do not use a standard form, your agreement should be a single document (not a file of letters) that is specific to that project, covering everything you have agreed to provide, what you will be paid and when.

Keep a separate fee file for the original signed fee agreement together with copies of all fee correspondence, file notes and submitted fee accounts. This will ensure that at any time you can immediately refer to this to deal with any fee issues or questions relating to the services to be provided by you. Keep it up to date at all times.

As the job proceeds your work will almost certainly be varied. If necessary, update your fee agreement to reflect the changed situation when the changes occur. Ensure you have confirmed in writing to your client all changes in your fee agreement with your client.

Other consultants and project managers

It is in your interests that other consultants (unless you are in a consortium situation) are always to be directly appointed and paid by the client and to have their own direct conditions of engagement.

You must ensure that if other consultants are to be employed – such as quantity surveyors, structural and services engineers, landscape architects and acoustic consultants – their general roles and to whom they are responsible, and how they relate to your role and responsibilities, are set out clearly.

If other consultants are appointed after you have started work, you must check your conditions of engagement to see how these new appointments affect your role and responsibilities. You must clarify with your client any uncertainties or ambiguities at that stage, not later when problems arise.

This applies particularly to the subsequent appointment of a project manager whose role will almost certainly impinge on your normal duties in preparing design and construction programmes, advising on and preparing contracts, and perhaps in some areas of your responsibilities to administer the building contract.

It is with this appointment particularly that many of the problems with gaps or overlapping responsibilities about 'who does what' and 'who is responsible to whom' situations arise.

While the client and the other consultants may not agree to you being advised of their fee structure, there is no reason why (and it is in the client's interests) you should not ask to see the other parts of these appointment agreements so that you can draw attention to any ambiguities or overlaps with their roles and responsibilities in relation to yours as the lead consultant and the supervising officer under the construction contract. This may also apply if it is decided to appoint a full-time clerk of works or if the client appoints their own contract supervisor.

Be clear as to your responsibilities; understand those of the other professionals involved and clarify any gaps or overlaps.

Form of fee agreement

Unless you or the client considers them inappropriate, use the standard RIBA forms of appointment, which are regarded as the industry norm, as the basis of your written fee agreement. If the client requires you to use their own bespoke form of appointment agreement, compare it with the RIBA terms and conditions and if necessary negotiate on points of divergence. Check with your PII provider that a non-standard appointment agreement is acceptable. (For further information refer to the RIBA Code Guidance Note 4 (Appointments).)

The selection of the appropriate RIBA Agreement depends on the complexity and the risks involved in a project. The four RIBA Agreements 2010 (2012 revision) are the Standard, Concise, Domestic Project and Sub-consultant conditions of appointment, and there are Consultants and Architects versions of each agreement. The RIBA agreements also cater for the difference in UK law in the treatment of consumers and business clients.

- A RIBA Standard Agreement 2010 (2012 revision) is suitable for a commission where detailed contract terms are required: the project should, in terms of value and complexity, merit the use of the JCT Standard or Intermediate forms of building contract or similar contracts. The Standard Agreement is compatible with a wide range of procurement routes (e.g. traditional, design and build). It is best used with a client acting for a business or for commercial purposes, although it may also be used for the construction of a client's home. Where the latter is the case the terms of the agreement should negotiated with the home owner client recognised under the law as a 'consumer'. A Standard Agreement comprises:

- Standard Conditions of Appointment
- the schedules of Project Data, Role Specifications, Design and Other services and fees and expenses.
- appendices, and
- a formal memorandum of agreement or letter of appointment.

- A Concise Agreement is suitable for a commission where the concise contract terms are compatible with the complexity of the projects and risks to each party. The Concise Agreement is suitable where building, extensions or alterations will be carried out using such forms as the JCT Minor Works Building Contract or the JCT Intermediate Form of Building Contract. It is best suited for clients acting for a business or for commercial purposes, although it may be used for a client's home where the terms have been individually negotiated. A Concise Agreement comprises:

- Concise Conditions of Appointment
- schedule of services
- schedule of fees and expenses
- any appendices, and
- a letter of appointment signed as a simple contract or as a deed under the seal.

- A Domestic Project Agreement is suitable where the commission relates to work to a client's home or where the terms are compatible with the complexity of the project. It is important that the contract terms are negotiated with the client as a consumer. A Domestic Project Agreement comprises:

- Domestic Project Conditions of Appointment
- schedule of services
- schedule of fees and expenses
- any appendices, and
- a letter of appointment signed as a simple contract or as a deed under the seal.

- A Sub-consultant Agreement is suitable where a consultant wishes to or is required to make an appointment of another consultant to perform part of his or her duties. It is best used where the contract terms are compatible with the agreement between the client and consultant. The agreement is not suitable for use by a client who intends to appoint specialist consultants directly.

Other components include:

- Access Consultancy Services Schedule 2012 (this schedule is for an experienced architect providing services in connection with the Disability Discrimination Act 1995)
- Contractor's Design Services Schedule
- Historic Building or Conservation Project Services Schedule

Supplementary Agreements include:

- Draft Third Party Schedule
- Draft Warranty by a Sub-consultant
- Public Authority Supplement.

If you must deal with the fee agreement by way of an exchange of letters or a client's own bespoke form of contract, do ensure they are carefully drafted and cover all the important areas relating to services to be provided by you and the fees to be paid. It is not good enough just to refer to the RIBA standard terms of appointment! The RIBA publishes the very useful *The Guide to Letter Contracts for very small projects, surveys and reports*.

In particular, as it is now general practice for appointments to be dealt with in stages, be careful where agreements cover partial services. Where does each stage start and finish? What is the commitment for your employment to continue during further stages? What are the implications for the copyright of your work? (See later in this section on how to deal with the copyright issue.)

If you are not registered for VAT at the time of making the agreement and you need to register for VAT as the project proceeds, make it clear that you will be obliged to add VAT at the appropriate rate on all fee accounts due from the date of your registration.

If you are presented by a developer client with their standard form of agreement, do not accept it without question. If it makes demands on you of which you are uncertain, negotiate to remove or amend those requirements. If it is complex, take legal advice before agreeing to sign.

The British Property Federation (BPF) produced in July 2007 the *BPF Consultancy Agreement (version 2.0)*, a standard consultancy agreement that the BPF considers applicable to all members of the professional design team. It has optional clauses to deal with the different roles of different professionals and also covers the different procurement routes.

The advantages of this agreement are that it includes third party rights, so avoiding the need for collateral warranties, and a clause covering novation. It envisages a 'lump sum' fee and that the consultant is only entitled to additional fees in certain defined circumstances. It is, however, an agreement drafted by clients and is considered by some to be very client biased.

If it is presented for you to sign, check it out if necessary with your PII provider and solicitors very carefully before you commit yourself.

If you have any doubts about any of these client agreements increasing your negligence liability, ask your PII provider to check and agree to any clauses that may relate to your PII cover. If they object to a requirement, you are in a strong position to negotiate with your client its removal or amendment – otherwise you will not have the PII cover they require, something the client will not want to agree to.

Watch out for wording that includes the requirement for you to 'ensure that' something is done when you can do no more than 'do your best' to do it.

Above all, be certain you can supply the service you are agreeing to provide within the time limits set by the client. This is a requirement of both the ARB and RIBA codes of practice (see Section 7).

Finalise the fee agreement and confirm it in writing before you start any significant amount of work. Check, and if necessary double-check, with your client what you have agreed to so that you avoid any possibility of misunderstandings or arguments later.

The 'moving goalposts' syndrome

A legal contract does not come into being until there is an offer and an acceptance. Without a binding contract you may have difficulty in getting paid. Binding contracts can be made orally, but these are invariably difficult to prove and enforce.

Avoid the 'moving goalposts' syndrome where, perhaps without realising it, you never actually finalise an agreement with your client. Unwittingly, or sometimes deliberately, just as you think you have agreed everything, they raise new issues to be negotiated and agreed, while you are pressing ahead with sketch designs and other work.

> The danger of allowing this situation to develop while carrying on with work is shown in the High Court decision on an architect's unsuccessful claim for fees against a 'domestic' client (the case of *Picardi* versus *Cuniberti* in 2002). The architect had confirmed what he considered to have been agreed with his client as the fee agreement, and although the client made no attempt to sign this he proceeded with his work until the relationship with the client broke down. An adjudication took place under which the architect was awarded substantial fees. This decision was challenged in the High Court, where the judge ruled that the client's failure to sign the architect's agreement was entirely deliberate and that the draft contract between the parties on which the architect had acted was of no effect. As a result, there was no authority for adjudication and the adjudicator's decision in favour of the architect was therefore invalid.

If you have a growing file of letters and notes of meetings relating to fee negotiations after you have started work on the project, beware: you are drifting into a 'moving goalposts' situation. If a client wishes you to start work before the fee agreement is finalised, agree a fee to cover a specified amount of preliminary work pending agreement and signing of the fee agreement.

You will have difficulty enforcing a contract that has not been finalised, for until there is an unqualified offer and acceptance there is almost certainly no enforceable contract.

If you lack a signed agreement, at best you will have to prove the terms of your oral agreement, and at worst you will not get paid at all!

Copyright issues

You own the copyright of your work – or do you?

Copyright is becoming an increasingly important issue when sites are sold with detailed designs and planning approvals and with design–build situations where another architect is employed to develop the original architect's design.

The architect's copyright

By law, as the architect, you own the copyright of your designs and drawings. This ensures that you can reproduce your original design on another site for another client. It prevents your client from reproducing your design on another site without your permission and paying you an additional fee for a licence to do so.

- Case law on copyright indicates that a marginal change to your design by another person is not enough to avoid you claiming a breach of your copyright.
- It is also possible (although difficult) to claim that unauthorised copying of a distinctive feature in your design is a breach of your copyright.

It is important not to give up your copyright when negotiating your fee agreement without fair and reasonable compensation. In many cases, for example with clients who build only once or very infrequently, there is no reason why your client should want to own your copyright or reproduce your design. *If you are designing houses for a speculative housing developer, the opposite will probably be the case.*

To avoid later problems, if your client wants to acquire your copyright, negotiate an appropriate additional fee at the outset. But do not give up your right to reproduce your own design unless it is unavoidable and you are properly compensated. You do not want to be in the position of being sued for reproducing your own design, whether in whole or a distinctive part.

While it may not be total protection against your copyright being infringed, include on all of your drawings and specifications:

> *[your name]* owns the copyright of this *[design/drawing/document]*, which must not be reproduced in whole or part without the written permission of *[your name]*.

This clearly draws your copyright ownership to the attention of your clients, and also to any third parties who may be tempted to use your design without your authority.

When employing 'contract' self-employed staff, ensure that you as the employer retain the copyright of all work produced by that person during their work in your office. Otherwise, at a later stage there could be a dispute as to who actually owns the copyright – you or the self-employed staff member. The employer – the individual architect, partnership or company – owns the copyright of design work carried out by 'employed' staff as the case may be.

Implied licence to reproduce your design

A client has an implied licence to use your design, for which they have paid you fees, in the construction of their building or extension on that site and no other. This is clearly set out in the terms and conditions of the RIBA Agreements.

Problems can arise when the site or building is sold on to a third party with the benefit of the planning approval for the building you have designed, or when your client decides to bring in a design–build contractor to complete your design without payment to you of any further fees. In both cases a new client or design–builder can claim the implied right to develop and build your design without further payment.

> *"If you have been paid a fee, that gives the client the right to sell your design."*

In general terms, the courts hold that providing your existing client has paid you a reasonable fee for the design work then they can transfer that implied right to a third party without further payment to you. That includes other architects employed by design–builders.

So do watch out for the not unusual situation where you agree a reduced fee to prepare a design and obtain planning approval. The client then sells on the site with the benefit of the design attached to the planning permission you have obtained, or employs a design–build contractor or another architect to work up and build your design without paying you any further fees.

If you have been paid a fee, that gives the client the right to sell your design on to a third party!

If you anticipate that your client may sell on the site once planning consent is obtained or may decide to use a design–builder, negotiate a clause in your agreement to ensure that, should this happen, you are either retained by the new owner at specified fees or paid an additional fee in compensation. A clause along these lines avoids you having to sue your client or third party for infringement of your copyright, where (assuming you were to win) the amount awarded would be relatively small. Instead, you sue on the much stronger ground of a breach of the contract term in your fee agreement.

Negotiate this when your client needs your skills to obtain planning approval. This should help you to agree a satisfactory clause that will avoid you being left without proper payment for using your creative abilities to obtain planning approval and so add value to the site. If you leave negotiation of this clause until after you have obtained planning approval or completed your design work, you are likely to get nothing.

"Protect your copyright interest with a contract clause that covers the payment to be made to you if the client sells the site or employs a design–build contractor without you being retained with agreed fees."

It is possible to obtain an injunction against someone who you are aware is going to breach your copyright. This has to be obtained before the breach has taken place, otherwise you will only be able to sue for damages; the amount that should reasonably have been paid to you in compensation for the breach. The danger with injunctions is that if the court subsequently decides your copyright was not about to be breached, you could face a big claim for damages from the other party.

Protect your copyright interest with a contract clause that covers the payment to be made to you if the client sells the site or employs a design–build contractor without you being retained with agreed fees.

Timing of fee payments

Cash flow is vital to financial stability and peace of mind, so you must plan your finances and your cash requirements against your projected fee income generally and job by job. Remember, businesses go bust because they run out of cash! A managed cash flow will keep the bank off your back by allowing you to keep within overdraft limits and will reduce interest charges. These may be tax deductible, but they still have to be paid out of profits.

So, agree with as much precision as possible when you will be paid. Link this to specific stages of your work so that when each stage is complete there can be no reason for you not to be paid on time for the work completed. Include the requirement for clients to sign off specific work stages, for which the related fee payments are to be made before you will start the next stage.

On all but small projects agree stage payments for the design and pre-contract phases. Agree regular, probably monthly, 'on account' payments during the long contract administration period. You then have a programmed and virtually guaranteed cash flow, which also reduces your fee exposure to those clients. As most problems arise during construction, this is a wise strategy!

Adjudication of disputes

Under the Construction Act as amended, a contract to provide consultant's services is a 'construction contract' and therefore must include provision for adjudication of disputes as they arise. If no adjudication clause is included in your fee agreement, the standard adjudication clause will apply. It is better for you and your client that you have an adjudication clause suited to your requirements than have imposed one that is more relevant to a building contract.

The Construction Industry Council publishes the *CIC Model Adjudication Procedure*, which if explained to your client should be acceptable.

Adjudication can be a very helpful way to get outstanding fees paid during progress without resorting to such draconian measures as suspending work. It is rapid, if rough and ready, justice, and not only works but also forces the client to pay, and the courts invariably support the adjudicator's decision. It can be challenged later, but unless large sums are involved this is unlikely.

However, there is no statutory right to adjudication on 'domestic' contracts. These are with clients who are owner-occupiers of the domestic property you are designing or extending. The standard terms and conditions of RIBA fee agreements include an adjudication clause automatically, but for this to be effective your 'domestic' client must agree to its inclusion. It is not sufficient merely to refer to this in negotiation or that it is in the agreement. To be certain it can be enforced you must draw your client's particular attention to the clause, explain its implications and obtain the client's agreement for it to be included. If you fail to do this the courts may set it aside.

Making payment easy

Establish at the earliest possible stage your client's system for paying accounts. Organise the timing of your fee applications to match your client's accounts department's procedures for paying bills. If they pay on the first day of the month and you send your account in on the second, you will not get paid that month! Obvious, but often overlooked.

Establish if they have a BACS system for making payments, and if so make sure they have your correct bank account details and inform them if these change for any reason. However, you may not notice when you have not been paid – you do not have the prompt of paying a cheque in to your bank. Do check that the BACS payments are being made on time, and that when paid they are recorded on the fee file.

With private clients, in particular, establish how they are funding the project and your fees. If they are raising a mortgage, establish with them in advance estimated amounts and timing of interim fee payments so that they can budget accordingly. A significant part of your fees will be due before building starts and they may overlook this.

Have a system to ensure you submit your accounts the moment they are due. If you have not sent an account to your client you cannot get paid! Submit your accounts in the format and timing that fits your client's established payment procedures and not your own. If you are not sure what they are – find out. It is hardly likely to be a secret!

Find out who will be responsible for approving your accounts and passing them for payment. This is the person you need to know well enough to make direct contact with when there are any problems or delays with fee payments.

You must also have a system for chasing unpaid accounts the moment they are overdue. It is good tactics for the initial payment chaser to be someone other than you. Keep it impersonal until the situation gets so difficult that you need to become involved. As the 'heavyweight', you go in when your normal chasing is not producing results.

Tactics such as sitting on a client's doorstep and refusing to move until you get your cheque may appear to be extreme, but can work. If you are told: 'I will put the cheque in the post tonight', say you will come over and collect it. The Royal Mail is sometimes blamed for not delivering important letters when they have simply not been posted!

If you have any doubt of the financial strength of the client, get the cheque specially cleared by your bank. Companies have been known to go into liquidation between the time the cheque was issued and the time it was cleared – or rather not cleared – by the bank.

If you are handing over drawings in return for an immediate payment of fees, consider insisting on a banker's draft rather than a cheque. Banker's drafts cannot be cancelled; cheques can be refused when presented by your bank.

Get your fee accounts out on time and in tune with your client's payments system, and have a system for chasing them if they are not paid on time.

Limit of liability

While you can and must cover your exposure to negligence claims with PII up to the affordable level, you are exposed to potential catastrophic claims that can be greater than your PII cover. It is wise, if possible, to negotiate a limit on your exposure to claims for negligence with your client when finalising your fee agreement.

If possible, agree that the level of your PII cover will be the limit of your personal, or company, liability to the client for that particular project. If this is to be included in your fee agreement then this clause must be fully explained to your client in advance so that they are aware of and agree to the implications. If you do not do this you could find the limit would not be enforceable if a claim should arise for a greater figure.

If the client requires higher PII cover, see if you can negotiate an additional fee to cover the extra premium involved. The limit of liability you agree in these circumstances should be at least an adequate and appropriate amount, as required by the ARB (see Sections 6 and 7). The RIBA agreements include the provision for insurance caps and net contribution clauses to limit your liability.

The BPF, as a client organisation, publishes a consultancy agreement intended to apply common terms and conditions to all consultants on a project. It is an open-ended contract which has no cap on liability and this could leave you without cover by your PII. The RIBA Practice Department advises against signing such an agreement unless you are fully aware of the conditions being imposed on you and have obtained the agreement of your PII provider to the conditions.

This is not a 'safe' agreement; you should avoid it if possible, only use it if it is acceptable to your insurer.

Termination

You will suffer financial loss if a client terminates their agreement with you without reasonable notice. You will have staff and overheads to pay, particularly if you have expanded your office to cope with the additional work on their project.

A large new project will involve you in start-up costs and increased overheads, which you will expect to recover from future fees. If your contract is terminated at an early stage, unless you have covered this in your fee agreement you will not recover those costs. Even termination occurring during preparation of production drawings or during construction can leave you with no work for staff for which you have financial commitments.

The RIBA Standard Agreement (Architect) covers termination fairly for both architect and client. If this form is not used as your agreement, ensure as far as you are able that any other form of agreement includes similar provisions. Check any client-drafted agreements carefully to ensure that the rights of termination included are fairly balanced between you and your client.

So, ensure that apart from small projects your fee agreement includes satisfactory arrangements for compensation for termination by the client for any reason other than your incompetence.

Interest on late payments

Late payments will cost you money. Make it less attractive for clients to delay payments by arranging to charge interest when payments are delayed beyond the agreed due date. Check if the provisions of the Late Payment of Commercial Debts (Interest) Act apply to you (if you have fewer than 50 full-time staff they almost certainly will) as they should give a statutory right to interest on late payments.

You may feel that your clients are unlikely to pay this, or that you would not wish to upset them, but even then it is useful to have made it clear that late payment interest will be due. If you do finish up with an adjudication or in court, the late payment interest can be included in your claim.

However, to enforce this clause you must be able to prove you are entitled to fees at that stage. This makes it all the more important to specify clearly in your fee agreement the amount and timing of your interim fee payments. There must also be no question that you have completed all the work required of you up to that stage.

When preparing fee accounts, add the date by which the account should be paid on the bottom, referring to the terms of the fee agreement, and include a note that interest at the statutory rate will be charged on overdue accounts.

As an incentive to pay by the agreed date, consider offering a discount on prompt payments of fees within, say, 30 days of being rendered. This can be attractive to smaller private clients, who will be spending their own 'after tax' money and for whom a discount will be seen as a real saving.

Expenses

To recover the total expenses incurred (prints, travel, etc.) you need to agree at the outset on what will be chargeable and ensure your office cost recording system follows this accurately.

If you agree a lump sum to cover all expenses, add a margin for error to ensure you are adequately covered. Expenses usually come out considerably higher than your 'guesstimate' made at a time when your instinct is probably to keep the figure as low as possible.

Keeping accurate records and receipts of chargeable and non-chargeable expenses on every job is essential. This is not only to ensure you recover the full amount of expenses due to you, but also as evidence of the level of expenses involved when negotiating a lump sum to cover expenses in fee agreements on comparable new jobs or with new clients.

If high cost 'extras' are required by the client (such as architectural models, virtual reality videos, etc.), make sure payments for these are the client's responsibility and ordered direct by them. If not, make it clear to them, and particularly with the model maker, that you are acting as the client's agent and not on your own account. Start your order with 'On behalf of my client … '. Otherwise, if the client does not pay, you may be held liable to pay the bills!

Novation

It is increasingly common for clients to appoint architects to design their building up to the detail design or contract stage and then transfer (novate) that architect to the contractor, who then becomes the client. Alternatively, you may be asked to act for a design–build contractor to prepare details and production drawings for a building designed by another architect. Also, it is now common practice for clients to sell a site or building with the benefit of your plans and the planning approval you have obtained to another person for them to carry out the development. This raises copyright issues, which are dealt with earlier in this section.

So, when negotiating your fee agreement, and particularly if you have earlier agreed a reduced fee for initial work, such as obtaining planning approval necessary for obtaining funding, and if there is any suggestion that your client may be considering selling the site with the benefit of your planning approval or the building, or 'novating' you to a design–build contractor at a later stage, then ensure you agree at negotiation stage how that situation is to be dealt with and what will be the fee to be paid to you and by whom.

You will almost certainly do a better deal then than later! You can argue with justification that it is in the client's best interests (as well as yours) to agree the terms on which this will take place as part of the fee agreement to avoid misunderstandings and problems later.

If you are novated to a design–build contractor by your existing client, do be careful that you avoid subsequent conflict of interest situations, such as retaining some duties and responsibilities to your first client. It is difficult, if not impossible, to work for two masters on the same project at the same time.

Do not agree to be novated until you are totally satisfied that the arrangements safeguard your fee and liability situations. Ensure you are not exposed to additional costs in the changeover to the contractor without proper reimbursement and that all your outstanding fees are paid. Novation can create significant liability problems, which are dealt with in Section 6.

Situations can arise where your original client agrees with you the fees you will be paid by the design–builder when novated. Do check when the novation is about to happen that the fees you agreed at the outset are appropriate to the work the design–builder will require you to perform.

Novation must be covered by a specific separate fee agreement with the design–builder, agreed and signed by your original client, the design–builder and yourself before you start working for the design–builder.

Keep a separate fee file!

You will need to refer to your fee agreement and relevant correspondence during the contract. Ensure they are readily available and not buried in general job files. This will enable you to refer quickly to your agreement when issues arise that impact on fees or costs. Also, it will allow you to check what was agreed at the outset and that changes are not occurring that should be notified and agreed with clients.

It is important to monitor the fee agreement constantly to ensure that changes that create additional chargeable work are noted at the time they occur. Notify your client immediately, not after the work has been carried out. This is particularly important where you have agreed a fixed price fee for a clearly defined service and you are being asked to carry out work over and above that which has been agreed.

Highlight in the file when you have a finalised fee agreement signed by your client. It will not only assist you when changes to your work or fees take place, but will also act as a reminder in the early stages that the agreement has not yet been finally agreed and so its provisions may not be enforceable.

When to get out? – before it is too late!

The most difficult decision to make is when to suspend or terminate your contract with your client and stop throwing good money after bad! Your client is not paying your fees and has become increasingly impossible to work with: time to get out!

If there are acute problems with payment, or relations with your client are becoming impossible, you need to withdraw rather than wait for the client to – rightly or wrongly – sack you. Be prepared to take the most difficult decision of all – to withdraw when you can no longer afford to work for that client. Cut your losses and walk away!

The Construction Act as amended gives you the helpful power to suspend work in certain situations, which was not always the case in the past. However, if possible, ensure the 'crunch' (when you make it clear you will not continue unless you are paid) comes at a time when your client needs you as much or more than you need them, not when they have all your drawings or the building is virtually complete or you are owed so much in unpaid fees that you cannot afford to walk away.

But remember that this may not apply if your client is a 'domestic' client – an owner-occupier of a domestic property. In those cases you will need to draw your client's specific attention to the clause in the relevant act and obtain their agreement to be certain you can enforce it.

In general, if you have completed the work you agreed to carry out for the client, you have the right in common law to retain the drawings until you are paid. You must, however, take legal advice before you terminate your contract or withhold from your client your drawings or other documents, for if your actions are found in the courts to be unjustified, considerable damages could be awarded against you in favour of your client.

Beware: the ARB's disciplinary committee has upheld some clients' complaints that their architects have abandoned them before completing their contracted services. If you walk away you may have to fully justify why. And if you cannot do this it could be you who's in trouble, rather than the client.

Speculative work: upside potential – downside risk

You have to speculate to a degree to obtain new clients and work. But too much speculative work can create workload and cash-flow pressures you can do without.

"Control the amount of speculative work you take on, and ensure that you are fairly recompensed for the risks you have shared with the client if it is successful."

So have a clear policy as to the proportion of your total workload you will carry out at risk before the project becomes fee earning or is abandoned. Avoid being drawn into a situation where you have completed so much work on a particular project or client that you cannot afford to cut your losses and walk away!

As a general principle, if your client is at risk it may be reasonable for you to take on an agreed degree of risk before being paid. If your client is not at risk, then why should you be?

Ask yourself what the consequences will be if none of the speculative projects come to fruition. Will you (a) have a headache, (b) have big problems or (c) risk bankruptcy? If (b), think hard before you get involved; if (c), you cannot afford the risk!

Make sure you assess in advance the upside potential – your rewards if the gamble comes off – and the downside risk – your losses if it collapses. It is OK to risk 10 per cent of your fee to earn the other 90 per cent, but not the other way round. If the risk you are expected to carry is total (no fees) or very high (nominal fee) then you need a fee reward to compensate you for the risk you are taking. It can be in a higher fee, a bonus or even, in certain circumstances, a share in the profits or equity of the scheme.

There is always a considerable risk of the site of a 'speculative' project being sold on to someone, who will then carry out the scheme, once the site or project has been obtained. You must plan for this eventuality when you first agree to become involved so that you will be compensated for the work you have carried out without payment and for your contribution to the success in obtaining the scheme.

So, establish with precision when you agree to work without being paid and the amount of work you will carry out at risk before the project becomes fee earning or is abandoned. If possible, agree at the outset the basis on which you will carry out further work when you reach the limit of the work you have agreed to do at risk.

You must avoid being drawn into a situation where you have done so much work that you cannot afford to withdraw and cap your losses!

Keep the amount of speculative work under control. Monitor the situation regularly. Do not let speculative work get out of proportion to, or have undue priority over, the fee-earning work that pays your bills. Ensure that your actual fee-earning work can support the cost of the speculative work for which you may not get paid.

You have to 'speculate to accumulate', but do so with care, and avoid being over-stretched financially or with staff resources such that your work on fee-earning work suffers. Make sure that one way or another you are properly recompensed for the time and expertise you have contributed and risked to win a speculative project.

Control the amount of speculative work you take on, and ensure that you are fairly recompensed for the risks you have shared with the client if it is successful.

Rainbow projects – the elusive pot of gold!

A multimillion pound project to drill for ink wells in China for a new client who is developing all over the world is too exciting to turn down! In reality, few such schemes come to fruition. The problem is that you get sucked in and find it almost impossible to decide when to cut your losses and get out.

So, avoid chasing rainbows! Be totally objective. How realistic is the 'on spec' project? How likely is it to become fee earning? How much can you risk in people and time before it does? If it goes ahead, will the fees you earn (assuming you get paid) justify the risk you have taken?

There is no point doing nine-tenths of the work on spec to earn the other one tenth if the project proceeds. Be clear when you will say 'Enough is enough', and refuse to carry out any more work without payment!

Getting paid!

Legal action to recover outstanding fees arises because you have not been paid the fees you are due. Obvious! So, your client's payment is overdue: but how much are you to blame for not getting paid?

You have not sent out your request for payment?
   Your fault? Certainly – if you do not send out a fee account you will not get paid!

You are not chasing payment?
   Your fault? If you do not chase overdue fees your client will probably pay someone else who *is* chasing them! The squeaking wheel gets the oil!

You are not performing?
   Your fault? Always check your client has no outstanding significant complaints about your service or the administration of the construction contract before sending out requests for fees! If there are problems, resolve them first if you can, and *then* send in your fee account.

There are contract problems?
   Your fault? If you have not kept your client fully informed and satisfied them that these problems are not of your making they will delay payment until they are satisfied. Disgruntled clients, justified or not, are reluctant to pay fee accounts until their complaints have been dealt with.

Misunderstandings over the service you were to provide?
   Your fault? Did you make absolutely sure there could be no misunderstanding over the service you would provide, the fees you were to be paid and when you would be paid and then confirm it in writing so that you would have evidence if needed?

Extra work ordered by the client?

Your fault? Did you ensure that client changes involving extra work and the additional fees were agreed and confirmed in writing before the work was carried out?

The client delays or refuses payment although they have no justifiable reason to do so?

Your fault? Before taking the job, did you check whether they had a good track record for paying people who worked for them on time? Should you have been aware they were going to be slow or non-payers?

The client does not have the means to pay?

Your fault? Did you check out their credit rating before agreeing to work for them and monitor the situation periodically?

SUMMARY

- Make sure you have a clear, unambiguous fee agreement *in writing* that establishes without question the services you are to provide and *what*, *when* and *how* you will be paid.
- Many problems with clients arise because of poor communication. Listen and understand what they are saying. Involve your clients in important decisions. Do not take responsibility for making decisions that should be made by your client. Confirm all client changes in writing. Avoid conflicts of interest and declare what may be considered to be potential conflicts of interest to avoid misunderstandings later.
- Make sure your agreement covers additional fees to be paid if the site is sold on or if a design–build contractor takes over implementation of your design.
- Carefully monitor the amount of speculative work you take on in relation to your fee-earning work. Have a clear understanding as to the amount of work you will carry out 'on spec' and make sure proper compensation is in place if the scheme proceeds and you are not retained as the architect.
- Set up procedures to ensure you get paid on time – chase late payments.
- Deal with clients' complaints as they arise, before they become major problems and possible negligence claims.
- Strive to keep your clients content at all times.
- Without clients, you have no work. Without fees, you have no practice!

Section 3
Keeping out of trouble by getting the building right

Architectural quality is subjective and debatable, but you cannot argue that a roof is not leaking when it is!

The client's brief

The client's brief is a vital starting point to achieving a successful and profitable project and satisfied clients. Many problems regarding design, construction and use of buildings stem from lack of, or errors and omissions in, the client's original brief.

Meeting your client's requirements is crucial to the success of your building and the goodwill of your client. Translating those requirements into an accurate and comprehensive client's brief is essential to meeting that objective. Without it, you will almost certainly be in for a very uncomfortable time.

As the project proceeds through its various stages, the client's requirements may change or have to be changed. When this happens consider the implications of the proposed changes in detail and search for unexpected problems elsewhere in the design and in the contract. Discuss the impact of these changes with your client, particularly the effect on design and construction decisions and any implications on time and cost.

If you need specialist advice from other consultants ensure your client authorise their use and is prepared to pay any additional costs.

Confirm agreed changes from the original brief in writing. With important changes, particularly those that will affect the work of others, update the brief and issue new copies to the other consultants involved, as well as to your client.

Assess the impact on your own work that will arise from the changes, and if the changes are being made by the client assess the amount of any additional fees or costs involved. Do not leave the agreement of extra fees until the end of the project. Even satisfied clients feel unhappy with unexpected additional fees or costs. So you will be at a disadvantage negotiating extra fees with them when the work is complete. Negotiation with a dissatisfied client at that late stage will be far more difficult!

Time spent on resolving as many aspects of the client's brief as possible at this early stage is always time well spent. It reduces the possibility of misunderstandings and client's changes of mind later. For you, as the architect, it provides a sound basis on which to start resolving the design problems posed by the client's requirements.

Defining the brief – sophisticated clients

Clients who have building programmes or who build regularly should have a clear idea of their requirements. They will probably provide you with a detailed brief specifying the building they require. Some will be comprehensive and very detailed, but watch out for those who will cover some aspects in great detail and leave gaps elsewhere. **What your client may not consider to be important may be a crucial design requirement to you.**

Establish whether anything is missing that should be included to ensure the brief covers all the issues you need to know at the outset. Check it against your own client's brief checklist to ensure you understand the full implications of their requirements and identify any gaps or inconsistencies that need to be resolved if uncertainties and problems are to be avoided later.

If necessary, have a question and answer session with the client (as early as possible) to resolve any doubts arising from their brief before you become too involved in the initial design process. Issues may be uncovered that have a profound effect on initial design considerations and possible solutions. It may also become clear that the job will require more work than you had anticipated, which you should take into account in your fee negotiations.

Ensure you get answers to your queries. If this is not possible, qualify your acceptance of your client's brief in writing to cover yourself against problems that may arise at a later stage. You may be wise to hold back on finalising your fee negotiations until you are satisfied that the brief covers all the issues that you consider must be included and that you need to be aware of.

Remember: while it is true that if things go wrong you may be able to argue that your client was an experienced developer and did not need your advice on that specific issue, it is far better not to be in a position where you have to use that as your defence against a claim.

Defining the brief – 'one-off' clients

The majority of clients do not engage in building operations frequently. For many it may be their first experience. They are likely to have only a general and incomplete concept of what they want and how much it may cost.

It is essential that you extract from these clients their requirements as to accommodation, time and cost and translate this into a written brief from which you can begin the design work. Send a questionnaire to the client to enable them to think through some of the issues in advance of a face-to-face question and answer session. This is important to enable you to clarify any uncertainties and obtain as precise instructions as possible as to their requirements.

If this exercise exposes the fact that the client's budget is significantly less that you (or the quantity surveyor) consider necessary to meet their requirements, this is the time to tell them and to confront and resolve the problem.

Remember: the courts invariably take the side of a 'lay' client if their claim is that you, as the expert, did not properly advise them in advance of the issue in dispute.

Client's brief checklist

The following is not intended to be a comprehensive checklist questionnaire. Rather, it covers most of the questions you need to ask to establish your client's brief. It will be helpful to also refer to *Construction Companion to Briefing* (RIBA Publishing). The questionnaire should include the following:

- **What** building does the client require?
- **When** will the client require the building?
- **How** much is the client prepared to pay?
- **What** will be the best procurement method?

Depending on the type of building and its complexity, the assistance of other professionals – particularly a quantity surveyor – may be required in drafting and dealing with sections of your questionnaire. On large or complex projects, you should advise the client which other consultants need to be appointed at this stage by them to help with the preparation of the brief.

What building does the client require?

What is the use of the building?

It is very important to establish the precise use of the building at the outset.

- Will the building be single use or mixed use in various parts?
- If mixed use, which parts will be used for what purpose and should these be interchangeable?

You need to avoid the risk of a claim of design negligence should the client subsequently change the use of the whole or part of the completed building and then claim it is not suitable for their changed use. For example, should all floor loadings throughout the building be the same or should some have a higher loading than normal for the general use proposed?

"Clients' use requirements often change over time. Do not get caught out by the claim that you should have anticipated the problem and dealt with it in your design."

Establish the client's use requirements at this stage to identify any potential problems with planning approval for the use or uses proposed. If necessary, make initial enquiries of the planning authority to establish there should be no problem in principle with either the use or uses proposed for a new building or change of use of an existing building.

With large buildings, fire protection may be a big issue. There may also be significant building regulation requirements, which may affect the design and cost. If this is the case, check out the ways to deal with it. Warn the client of any significant design or cost implications at this stage. If necessary, qualify the brief to cover yourself against this arising later and your client claiming that you should have warned them of this problem in advance.

Clients' use requirements often change over time. Do not get caught out by the claim that you should have anticipated the problem and dealt with it in your design.

What is the size of the building?

Make sure you ask the following questions:

- How big is the building or extension the client has in mind?
- Can it be comfortably accommodated on the site available?
- What is the site cover?
- Are there any height restrictions?
- Is visual bulk an issue?

In addition to the practical considerations, you must consider the visual and/or structural relationships with adjoining buildings.

- Will it create significant problems in obtaining planning approval?
- Can potential objections from the planning control authorities and/or adjoining owners be overcome without later substantial and costly design or construction changes?

If you instinctively feel that it will be very difficult, perhaps impossible, to design a building of the size or nature the client wants within the client's total budget figure then bite the bullet at that stage – not later when the client may be saying to you 'but you should have warned me of that before you made me spend all that money on your fees'.

Identify and warn your clients at this stage of any significant potential problems and decide with your clients how and when you will deal with them. Do not crash on regardless and hope for the best! The best rarely happens in these situations.

Site boundaries

It is surprising how many projects get into trouble through uncertainties and problems with site boundaries. If problems with boundaries are not discovered until after you have started building, you may have a very expensive problem to resolve.

So do obtain a site plan from your client (it may be a copy of their Land Registry title plan) which defines clearly the boundaries of the site on which you are to design their building. Check your site survey against this plan.

Check with your client the ownership of boundary walls and fences. If a hedge, is the boundary on the centre of the hedge? If not, where is it?, and who owns the hedge? If there are any uncertainties, advise your client to resolve them with the adjoining owners. You must avoid your client and you getting caught up in a neighbour dispute.

Restrictive covenants

You need to know at an early stage if there are any restrictive covenants on your client's site or building that may need to be taken into account in your design and layout. Get your client to check their title deeds, if necessary through their solicitors. If there are restrictive covenants, it is not within your expertise to decide whether they are unenforceable and can therefore be ignored. It is a decision for their solicitors, not for you.

If there are enforceable restrictive covenants, ensure that both your design and the construction contract take these into account. If they relate to site boundaries, check their impact with your client's solicitors.

Land subject to subsidence or contaminated by previous uses

In areas where there is mining or where mining has taken place in the past, check local records to see whether it has at any time taken place under your client's site. If it has, it is for a structural engineer to advise on whether any special requirements are necessary for dealing with potential subsidence problems.

Check with the local authority (and if necessary the Environment Agency) whether there are any records of previous uses that may raise possible issues of contaminated land, which may have to be dealt with before you can start building.

If you have any doubts on these issues, advise your client that a site investigation is necessary to avoid what otherwise may be costly additional work and delays at a later stage.

Flood prevention

High-profile severe flooding of built-up areas has resulted in tighter regulation of building on known flood plains. In areas zoned as high risk, some forms of new development will not be approved. Check with the local authority and/or the Environment Agency whether your client's site is within a flood plain. If it is, establish at an early stage any restrictions or special precautions that you may have to take account of in your design.

Shell and core building?

The client may require a 'shell and core' contract for the main structure and fabric of the building followed by a separate fit-out contract. If so, ask the following questions:

- Where will the demarcation line be drawn?
- How will the fit-out contract be handled?
- Will the fit-out contract be the responsibility of the potential tenant?
- If not, who will be responsible?
- Establish a procedure for early discussions between yourself and whoever is responsible for the design and construction of the fit-out contract to avoid design conflicts and additional costs.

The dividing line between the shell and core contract and fit-out contract will be important. Make sure you get the fit right.

Flexibility and future extensions?

Is maximum or selective flexibility of use and layout to be designed into the building? Flexibility invariably costs extra so make clear to your client at an early stage the extra costs likely to be involved. If necessary get the client to agree to an initial study to establish what those extra costs will be and whether they can be justified.

Is the client likely to need to extend the building in the future? If so, how would this be accommodated? Will the extensions be horizontal or vertical? Bigger floors or more floors? What are the cost implications now and in the future? Should planning approval be obtained for the ultimate building size now with the building constructed in stages, or is it better left until the extension is required?

This future extension should be part of your future workload.

Vehicular access and servicing?

Access can be a particular problem, both in practical and planning terms. You must therefore discuss the requirements with the client.

- Will the site require oversized lorry access?
- What are the requirements for parking areas for staff and visitors and private car parking for owners?
- Are there likely to be any problems with obtaining planning approval for access from adjoining roads?

- Will there be restrictions on or requirements for car parking?
- Will these be significant problems?
- Can the problems be overcome and will the potential restrictions be acceptable to your client?
- Will it be possible to resolve the problems in ways acceptable to your client and within their total budget cost?

If the vehicular service areas do not work properly, you and your client have problems.

Special requirements?

Make sure you know of any special requirements for the building.

- What clear floor heights are required?
- What are the number and shape of floors?
- What clear spans are needed?
- Are there any restrictions on structural subdivisions?
- What floor loadings are required?
- Will floor loadings be variable or consistent throughout the building?
- Are raised floors required for IT or other purposes?
- Are suspended ceilings required for essential services?

Ensure the client tells you about any unusual requirements that may not be immediately obvious and are not in your questionnaire.

Remember: what you may consider to be an unusual requirement they may think is obvious, which is why they may say they did not mention it!

Life span of the building?

You must know how long the client wants the building to last: 30 years? 60 years? 125 years? forever? A retail shed is not expected to last as long as (or cost as much as) a museum!

Life span can be a significant issue in the design, the quality of materials used, the methods of construction and, of course, in the final cost! Long-life buildings are usually more expensive because the materials and systems used are invariably more costly than with buildings expected to last no longer than say 30 or 60 years. The life expectancy of your building has implications not only on initial construction costs but also on short- and long-term maintenance and refurbishment costs.

So agree with the client at brief stage the life expectancy of the building you are to design. Ensure they understand that long-life materials and short-cut construction methods are invariably more expensive (and will probably add to the building time) than cheaper short-life solutions.

"In olden days buildings were intended to last forever and often did. Not so today."

In olden days buildings were intended to last forever and often did. Not so today.

Client's 'nomination' of specialists or materials?

Some clients, for their own good reasons, wish to ensure that certain materials, products and specialists are used in preference to others. Establish which of these may have significant cost or time implications. Include these as part of the client's brief as they may affect your design decisions. If they involve specialist firms who will have an input into your design, you need to know at this stage. All nominations will need to be fully and accurately incorporated in production drawings and specifications and particularly in the tender and the contract documents.

Also check any potential delivery problems with major items to be specified by the client. When construction industry activity is high, some major building components – lifts for example – can go out to very long delivery times and may have to be ordered in advance of placing the main building contract.

Discourage clients from appointing separate specialist contractors who will not be under your control and warn them of the potential problems, particularly if the specialist contractor will need to start work on site before the main contract has reached practical completion. Also, warn of any potential insurance problems with two separate contractors working on the site at the same time.

As nomination creates responsibility and legal complications in the building contract, encourage your clients to avoid nominating separate outside contractors unless there are very special reasons to go down that route.

Services, heating, lighting?

Make sure you know your client's needs for services.

• Is the building to be naturally ventilated or air conditioned?

- What telephone, computer and other internal and external communication systems are specified?
- Are any other specialist services required?
- How crucial to the client (or occupier) are running costs and their sustainability policy?

You also need to know:

- Who will be responsible for design and installation?
- Will there be in-house input from the client?
- Will specialist professional consultants be appointed by the client to be responsible for these areas?
- If so, will the consultant be responsible to you as the architect?
- If not, to whom will they be responsible?

If the finished building cannot properly accommodate your client's technology requirements you will have problems.

Quality of the finished building?

Make it clear that the generally accepted 'normal' quality standard will be provided unless the client instruct you to specify a higher standard. You will have to find out from the client whether any special fittings, finishing or furniture will be required above the normal standard expected for this type of building. If they are, ensure that standard is reflected in budget cost estimates and is carried right through to the contract documents, details, specifications and work on site.

The courts generally take the view that if clients are paying for a top-of-the-range Rolls Royce finish, that is what they are entitled to. So, if it is to be a bargain-basement basic Ford finish, make sure that is agreed in the brief at the outset.

When novated to a design–builder, remember they are now your client to whom you are legally responsible. Do not agree to retain a responsibility to your original client to check that the quality of materials or methods used by the contractor are as specified in your original design. You will have a serious conflict of interest if you become aware that the specified standard is being lowered to save cost or speed up construction. You cannot serve two masters at the same time and it is very unwise to put yourself in that position!

Wherever possible, establish quality standards with the client. Include them in the contract documents by reference to acceptable existing examples, which can be used as quality benchmarks. Check these benchmarks will still be in place during and after your contract period. If necessary, have sample panels constructed at the outset to set the standard in stone. But be sure the standard you require is possible to achieve in practice.

Above all, ensure that the materials, products and workmanship you subsequently select and specify will meet the quality standards agreed with the client at this stage. If the client subsequently increases their quality requirements as the design develops ensure you warn them of any increased costs or any supply delays when they make that decision, not later when the embarrassing problems that stem from their decision surface.

If clients think they are not getting what they are paying for, you have problems.

Project funding?

Few building projects are funded directly from the client's own financial resources. So find out:

- Who will provide the funding?
- Will they have any special requirements on payment stages and issue of certificates?
- Will the funder be involved in design or construction contract decisions?
- If so, what will be the extent of their involvement?
- How will this be controlled?
- Who will be the person responsible within the funder's organisation you will need to liaise with during the design and construction stages?
- Will you be expected to sign warranty or other third party agreements?

You will also need to know whether the contractor will be asked to provide funding for the development. Contractors with dual roles as part clients and builders may cause problems unless their role and responsibility as part clients are well defined in advance. If you are only made aware of a funder's involvement and requirements at a later stage this will create administrative and cost problems for everyone, including you as the architect.

He who pays the piper calls the tune: make sure this is established at the beginning, not half way through.

Lifetime operating costs?

You must know how important it is to the client to reduce maintenance and running costs to the minimum, bearing in mind that these aims usually result in higher capital cost at the outset.

Funding institutions and long-lease tenants of buildings are now an increasing influence over design decisions that relate to long-term maintenance costs. If the client has already made arrangements with institutional funders or occupiers, make sure they establish with them and you at briefing stage any specific requirements on the design or construction of the building that should be included in the brief. You and possibly your clients will have problems if these are bounced on you later.

With Private Finance Initiative (PFI) projects, where the bidding consortia take on the responsibility for operating and maintaining the building for up to 30 years, the costs of operation, moving parts replacement and long-term maintenance over that period are increasingly important. This situation is increasingly the case on other major projects.

In the past, long-term maintenance was rarely considered. Today it can be an important part of your client's brief.

When will the client require the building?

A few years after completion, the time taken to design and construct the building may have been forgotten. However, it will usually be a very important issue during design and construction, therefore at the earliest possible stage establish the client's requirements as to a target date for occupation of the building.

- Is it realistic?
- Is there any flexibility?
- Is time of the essence?

You must determine whether the target date is likely to be achievable when taking into account:

- possible planning approval delays
- site availability
- your ability to design within the time frame
- the contractor's ability to complete the building
- time required to commission the building after completion.

This is the time for you to identify any doubts and resolve the issues – not later!

Draw up an outline timetable identifying the likely timing for:

- design
- planning approvals
- detailed design
- contract placement
- construction period
- main completion
- fitting out
- commissioning
- client occupation.

Identify the areas of greatest uncertainty, which may cause cost or delay problems, and those which can be accelerated if necessary, emphasising to your client any cost implications that may be involved.

Always include a realistic time scale for obtaining planning and other statutory approvals. Experience shows that even simple planning approvals invariably take longer than anyone originally anticipated.

Having agreed an outline programme with the client, it is essential that all involved, including other consultants, are aware of this and the crucial dates which, if missed, will significantly change the programme or anticipated final completion date. Attach a copy of the outline programme to the final brief agreed with the client.

As soon as possible, translate these requirements into a bar chart that clearly shows the operations and decisions crucial to achieving the target dates. Make sure everyone involved is aware of the agreed programme and how they fit into the design process. Update the chart throughout the design stage, and eventually incorporate this into an agreed programme with the chosen contractor.

Most importantly, monitor the programme at all stages. If problems arise warn the client in good time so they can take any necessary decisions to avoid or mitigate the effects of the problem that has arisen.

If the client's target completion date is unrealistic, say so at this stage. Later may be too late!

Staged completion?

Establish with the clients whether they require staged completion and handover of parts of the building in advance of completion of the contract. If so:

* What is the required sequence?
* Will the phasing be practical?
* Will it create problems with planning and other statutory approvals?
* Will the planners include stringent conditions in the planning approval that the building cannot be occupied until certain parts have been completed and are in operation?
* Will the phasing create additional costs or delay the final completion?
* Are these costs or delays acceptable to the client?

Apart from the contract issues with delays, disruption and costs, taking over part of a building before completion also creates difficulties with building and third party insurances and health and safety issues which need to be anticipated and dealt with in advance.

If staged completion is required, or may be needed, agree the impact of this on your work and what is to be included in the contract to deal with these as early as possible.

Staged completion imposed on a contractor at a late stage will cause problems for everyone and will almost certainly result in extra costs for your client.

Site availability?

Check (and double-check) with the client the availability of the whole of the site for the start of building work. Once the contract is placed, late delivery of even part of the site not only delays completion but can also expose the client to substantial contractor claims for delay and disruption.

In urban developments, dealing with adjoining owners agreements, such as party walls, can cause delay, disruption and additional costs if the contract has already started on site. Deal with these wherever possible well before the contract is placed and include a realistic time in the initial programme as they can otherwise delay starting work on site. If the contract has already been placed with a start date that then has to be delayed, your client will not be pleased!

Do not allow your client to be committed to a start on site when there is any chance they may not be able to deliver access to the whole of the site to the contractor by the time in the contract.

Project managers – help or hindrance?

Project managers, if appointed, are invariably involved with design and construction programmes. If the project manager acts as no more than a post office between you, the client and others, you will have problems. But competent project managers, with clearly defined roles and who do not usurp your authority as the architect, should help you have a satisfactory building on completion, and a happy client! Many large clients now appoint a project manager to be responsible for the project from the earliest stage, and who may advise the clients on a number of issues, including whether you are the architect to be appointed. Beware. Their influence cannot be ignored.

With project managers increasingly being appointed by clients to oversee the whole of the design and construction process, some of the architect's traditional responsibilities may be passed on to the project manager.

If the client has appointed a project manager before you are appointed, resolve these issues when you are negotiating your appointment and fee agreement. Make sure the respective roles and responsibilities of you and the project manager are set out and confirmed in writing. In particular, ensure you know:

- What are the project manager's role and responsibilities in relation to yours as the architect and supervising officer under the contract?
- What are the project manager's responsibilities in relation to the other professional consultants employed by the client?
- Who is to be responsible for preparing and updating the project programme?
- Who is responsible for keeping the client informed of all significant changes and any problems that may arise?
- If it is you, do you report direct to the client or through the project manager?
- As the architect, do you still retain prime responsibility for co-ordinating the work of the other consultants into the overall pre-contract and post-contract programmes?

If there is any confusion or uncertainty between your responsibilities as the architect and the those of the project manager there will be problems.

How much is the client prepared to pay?

Your client's budget?

In the end, all construction disputes, whether they are during construction or in the High Court, are about money. Many client complaints about architects to the ARB and the RIBA include allegations that the architect has exceeded, or allowed the project to exceed, the budget cost made clear at the outset by the client as the maximum cost that should not be exceeded.

Establish at the outset your client's contemplation of their total budget costs, including professional and statutory fees.

- How realistic are the estimates that make up this total cost?
- How sensitive to cost is the project?
- Can a reasonably accurate 'guesstimate' of project cost be made at this initial stage?
- Will this estimate fit into the client's budget figure?

If it is clear that the client's cost budget is unlikely to be sufficient for the building they

"Do not just blunder on and hope it will come all right in the end. It rarely does!"

require, taking into account what has been established in the answers to the client's brief questionnaire, now is the time to address the problem. Persuade the client to either increase the budget or reduce the requirements for the building.

So, establish agreed cost parameters with the client at the outset and keep the client fully informed, confirmed in writing, of any matters that arise which may increase the final building cost beyond the agreed budget cost.

If the cost budget is so unrealistic that it is clear it cannot be achieved and the client is not able or prepared to increase it to a realistic figure, act now, not later.

Do not just blunder on and hope it will come all right in the end. It rarely does!

Client's cash flow?

Your client needs to be sure that the cash demands of the project match their availability of cash. Provide the client with a provisional cash-flow estimate, show- ing timings and approximate amounts of payments for planning and statutory approvals, to yourself and other consultants for interim fees, and, with the help from the quantity surveyor, to meet contractors' certificates during construction. A client's inability to pay contractors' certificates on time is a potentially very serious situation.

Clients do not like surprises, particularly if they do not have the cash required immediately available. But be careful how you word such client advice. If quantity surveyors are employed, they are the people to provide this information at your client's request. If not you need to get your client to agree to you consulting a quantity surveyor and to be responsible for the additional costs involved.

If the client requests an accurate estimate at that stage, your advice should be that they appoint a quantity surveyor to provide financial information that is beyond the professional expertise of you as the architect. If no quantity surveyor is to be appointed, be careful to qualify that any guidance you give can be no more than a broad assessment at that early stage, which will need to be monitored as the project develops and checked with the contractor before the contract is signed.

You should have agreed with your client when negotiating your appointment the timings of your interim fee payments. Again, advise your client if these change significantly as the project develops.

If your client does not have the cash to pay you, you have a problem: if the client does not have the cash to pay contractors, you all have problems!

Architect's interim certificates?

An estimate of the value of interim certificate payments should be discussed with the contractor before the contract is signed. This will ensure your client understands from the outset the frequency of your interim certificates and that these must be paid within the contract time limits. Provide your client with up-to-date cash-flow projections to avoid any significant changes from previous estimates, which might embarrass your client financially.

Challenged or incorrect interim certificates are a frequent factor in negligence claims.

Third party warranties?

Third party warranties are often required to enable third parties, such as those who may have funded the project or who occupy the building when completed but who are not party to the construction contract or the contracts with the architect and other designers, to recover damages from those parties. As a third party, with no contract with you, they have to rely on claims in tort to claim damages from you for professional negligence.

Although the Contracts (Rights of Third Parties) Act 1999 enables some third parties to sue directly for negligence damages, third party warranties are still at times required by many developers and the occupiers of their buildings. They effectively create a direct 'duty of care' liability between you and those third parties who are involved in some way with your building but with whom you do not have a direct contract liability, as you do with your client.

If your client requires you and the other professionals and contractors to provide funders, purchasers and future occupiers of the buildings with design and construction warranties, you should establish this when negotiating your fees and agreeing the client's brief.

Your client will have a problem, and you will be embarrassed, if at a later stage they attempt to insist on you signing warranties that you were not committed to at the outset as part of your appointment agreement. It is in both your best interests and those of your client to deal with these issues at the outset, not later.

The British Property Federation's *BPF Consultancy Agreement*, which is intended to apply common terms and conditions to all consultants on a project, does not require consultant warranties although it has provisions for Third Party Rights. The RIBA Practice Department advises against signing such an agreement unless you are fully aware of the conditions being imposed on you and have obtained the agreement of your professional indemnity insurance (PII) provider to the conditions. This is an open-ended contract which has no cap on liability.

If you are asked to sign warranties, you must check with your PII provider that the terms are acceptable to them and that any additional liabilities you are taking on are covered by your PII policy. Most developers, where they require warranties, use standard forms so this should not be a problem, but always obtain your PII provider's agreement in writing before you sign. Otherwise you could find yourself not covered by your PII should there be a claim. That will be in nobody's interests, least of all your client's. That is usually a persuasive argument against your client attempting to impose terms unacceptable to your PII provider on you.

If you are asked to sign a design warranty, ask your client to confirm that the other design consultants employed by them are obliged to sign similar warranties to cover their work. The warranty may include a clause listing deleterious materials that should not be specified or used in the building. Check the clause and ensure it only includes materials that are known to be potentially harmful, and that you are only expected to use reasonable skill and care in selecting materials based on the state of knowledge at the time you specify.

A warranty should be limited to no more than 12 years from the completion of the building, in line with the normal time limits in contract law.

Do not enter into any warranties if you can avoid them. If unavoidable, check with your PII provider and if necessary take your own legal advice before agreeing to sign.

What will be the best procurement method?

Traditionally, there was only one procurement route: detailed design by the client's professional team, competitive tenders and a standard JCT building contract, with the contractor responsible for building what others had designed.

However, while that route is still used in the majority of small to medium-size projects, particularly those for 'domestic' clients, a wide variety of alternative procurement routes are now available, with options to suit particular client needs and situations.

An initial decision on procurement should be made when preparing the client's brief, accepting the possibility there may be changes later. Ideally, it should be decided at this stage, with a changed final decision if necessary made later. It will also give you a clearer picture as to your client's intentions regarding, say, a possible switch to a design–build contractor and, if so, whether you will be retained by the client as their watchdog, novated to the design–build contractor, or left high and dry. If discussed at this early stage it will be very helpful to you and will enable you to anticipate these possibilities and your terms of appointment when you are negotiating your fee agreement.

Careful consideration of the alternatives at the earliest possible stage will be helpful, although the final decision and as a result the form of contract to be used will be made later. The more detailed issues and potential problem areas are dealt with in Section 4.

Broad considerations to be covered at the client's brief stage are likely to be:

- How is the risk that is inherent in any construction project to be shared between the client and the contractor? This varies considerably depending on the procurement route and contract form chosen.
- Is time to be of the essence? If so, a procurement method that ensures rapid completion on time will be essential.
- Is minimum cost essential? The traditional route will probably be best for achieving lowest construction cost, although that is not always necessarily the case. Sufficient time must be allocated for the design and preparation of tender and contract documents before tenders are invited, otherwise the building cost on the contract documents will bear little resemblance to the final cost of the project due to claims for delay and disruption as a result of changes and late information.
- Will the client want to keep close control of detailed design development? A traditional or perhaps management contracting route may be best in this instance. Almost certainly a design–build contract is unlikely to be the best route as the client loses complete control over detailed design.
- Is guaranteed final cost without extras essential? If so, design–build may be the answer, provided the client knows what they require, has an accurate and comprehensive set of employer's requirements and does not subsequently change their mind!

Standard client's brief checklist

Develop your own standard checklist based on the above considerations for use as a basis for establishing your clients' briefs. Add to and change it as experience indicates to cover all clients and building types. Use this to check the briefs provided by the sophisticated clients and as a basis for a questionnaire to 'one-off' clients.

Establishing the right brief at the earliest stage is an essential ingredient in the creation of a building that meets the client's requirements, gives satisfaction to all involved and avoids many later problems that are endemic in the design and construction process.

Time spent on establishing the client's brief in as much detail as possible and then recording it in writing and monitoring it during the progress of the project and confirming those changes in writing to the client will always be time well spent.

SUMMARY

- The client's brief is crucial to the success of your building. Time spent getting the client's requirements – the brief – right is never wasted.
- With one-off, unsophisticated clients, develop a questionnaire that will enable you to obtain the information you require as to what, when and how much, to enable you to prepare the brief.
- Carefully check a detailed design brief given to you by a sophisticated client who builds frequently to ensure it includes all the information you require and that there are no unacceptable requirements.
- Confirm the brief in writing and monitor it constantly for subsequent client changes.
- Establish the most suitable procurement method and form of contract to meet your client's brief.

Getting the right brief is the key not only to a successful and profitable project but also to keeping you out of trouble later on.

Section 4
Keeping out of trouble with building contracts

The seeds of problems to come may have been sown earlier, but the consequences will bring trouble to you during the contract stage. Building contracts are littered with tripwires to fall over – and people waiting to trip you up!

You have your client and your fee appointment and you have agreed the client's brief. Now for the really difficult part – getting the client's building completed on time and within budget.

The most likely areas to cause you problems will be:

- use of an inappropriate form of contract
- not having sufficient time to develop your design before tenders are invited
- contract documents that do not match the accepted contractor's tender
- starting on site before you (and other consultants) can issue sufficient completed construction information to ensure that you will not delay the contractor and face disruption and delay claims
- not having explained the terms and obligations to your client before they sign the construction contract.

Which contract?

Discussions held when drawing up the client's brief (Section 3) should have established the most likely procurement route to be followed and the probable form of contract to be used.

The tender documents, on which the contract cost will be based, must specify which standard form of building contract is to be used. You should have established with the client at briefing stage, or as the design was developed, the most appropriate standard contract to be used to meet the client's requirements, and now is the last chance for you and your client to review that decision.

So, before preparing tender documents, review the procurement situation. Explain to your client the various standard contract forms available and the merits and disadvantages of each of the alternatives. Make your client party to the decision as to which is the most appropriate form to use on their project. If they are 'lay' clients you must ensure they understand the options. It is their contract, not yours.

The most up-to-date suite of contract forms from the Joint Contracts Tribunal, the JCT 2011, provides a wide choice. While it may be tempting to continue to use older versions of JCT contracts, this will be dangerous as they will not be updated to deal with legal decisions or practice changes and will become out of date in a relatively short time.

Use the wrong form or one that you do not fully understand and you will have a very uncomfortable contract to administer.

JCT contracts for large complex projects, likely to be used or recommended by architects

- **JCT 11 Standard Building Contract With Quantities (SBC/Q)**

    This is the JCT contract form you are most likely to recommend to a client for large and complex contracts.

    Be fully aware of the inter-related sub-contract forms intended to be used in conjunction with the main contract.

- **JCT 11 Standard Building Contract Without Quantities (SBC/XQ)**

    You need good reasons to recommend to a client the use of a contract form for large complex projects that does not require the contract price and final cost to be established with priced bills of quantities. Unless you have an in-house quantity surveyor, you should recommend the client appoints their own quantity surveyor to deal with valuation and agreement of variations and interim and final certificates. As an architect, you are unlikely to have the specialised expertise to deal with cost and valuation matters. Do not venture into areas where you do not have the specialised expertise.

    Do not recommend the use of this contract form to clients unless there are good reasons to use it rather than the full quantities version and your client fully understands the reasons for its use and the risks involved.

■ JCT 11 Standard Building Contract With Approximate Quantities (SBC/AQ)

You need to have even better reasons for recommending the use of a contract that will rely on approximate (quick) bills of quantities to establish the contract cost. The client will not have a firm contract cost figure at the outset and will need to rely on remeasurement after completion to know the final cost.

If your client is considering this form, question why? Is it to save time? To make an earlier start on site? Are those sufficient reasons for not having a full bill of quantities? Are there other procurement routes that will meet those requirements with greater final cost certainty for the client?

JCT contracts that are most likely to be used or recommended by architects working on smaller, less complex projects

■ Minor Works Building Contract (MW)

This is a simple contract form with a proven track record in use, which can be used or recommended for small, simple projects. Do not be tempted to use it on larger, more complex projects.

If in doubt, use the JCT intermediate (IC).

■ Minor Works Building Contract With Contractor's Design (MWD)

This contract form is similar to the Minor Works Building Contract but with the facility for contractors to be responsible for parts of the design.

The minor works form is intended for works 'of a simple character'. In the past, architects developed the habit of using the old, 1998 minor works form while at the same time leaving some specialised design work to the contractor or specialist supplier (such as roof trusses and prestressed concrete floors), and for this reason the contractor's design facility was added to the form. This enables the architect to make the contractor responsible for these elements.

Nevertheless, do be careful if you decide to use this minor works form. It should be possible for the architect to design, detail and specify all of the work involved in minor works without undue difficulty within the time available. If specialist design is required, is this the most appropriate form to use?

Be careful. Only use the minor works form with contractor's design if there are very good reasons to complicate what has been a very successful simple contract form.

If you have any doubts, use the intermediate form with contractor's design (ICD).

■ Intermediate Building Contract (IC)

This form is intended for use 'where the proposed building works are of simple content involving the normal, recognised basic trades and skills of the industry, without building service installations of a complex nature or other complex specialist work'.

That being so, it may be dangerous to use or recommend this contract as an alternative to the main JCT contract SBC/Q. If In doubt, use SBC/Q!

It is safer to consider this contract as the alternative to using the JCT Minor Works Contract (MW) where you have doubts that because of the size and complexity of the work the minor works form may not be adequate for you to adequately administer the contract.

This is a well-used contract that bridges the gap between small, very simple projects and those that need the complex, major works forms.

■ Intermediate Building Contract With Contractor's Design (ICD)

This contract form is similar to the Intermediate Building Contract (IC) but includes provision for contractors to be responsible for parts of the design.

Do not be tempted to use this variation of the intermediate form to enable you to pass off design responsibility to the contractor. The form is intended to be used 'where the proposed building works are of simple content involving the normal, recognised basic trades and skills of the industry, without building service installations of a complex nature or other complex specialist work'.

That being so, before using this form ask yourself why you or the client should need the contractor to be made responsible for the design of portions of this building?

■ Building Contract for a Home Owner/Occupier who has appointed a consultant to oversee the work (HOpack)

This contract is primarily for use for small alteration and extension contracts where a consultant (architect) is appointed by the client, who is a 'domestic' client, in the traditional way. Be very careful if you consider recommending its use for new-build projects. It does have the benefit of a Crystal Mark award from the Plain English Campaign, but experience is that the use of plain English does not prevent lengthy arguments by lawyers as to the interpretation of what particular 'plain English' words such as 'reasonable' actually mean.

As virtually all home owner/occupier clients will be 'lay' clients, they are unlikely to be telling you which contract to use. Before recommending the use of this 'consumer' form, be clear as to its merits for the client compared with the minor works form.

Do discuss with your client the merits of this small works form compared with the JCT minor works form so that they understand the merits or disadvantages and agree with the final selection of the form to be used.

- **Building Contract for a Home Owner/Occupier who has not appointed a consultant to oversee the work (HOB)**

This form, first introduced in 1999, covers the situation where architects, while designing the contract work, do not want to be involved in the construction stage. It is also for use where clients wish to reduce the architect's fees and manage the work themselves.

However, while there are advantages in you not being involved in the construction work – it is the least profitable part of your work and carries the highest risk – be careful how you advise your client to use this form. Design and construction can never be totally separated, and if thing go wrong you may not be able to avoid getting drawn into the ensuing dispute.

When using this contract form, make sure your clients are fully aware in advance of the risks they are taking on in entering the jungle of construction work and managing a contract without a professional.

Other JCT contract forms

There are a wide variety of other JCT forms available for dealing with the alternative procurement routes now in use. These forms are more likely to be used by 'sophisticated' clients who develop or build regularly and who will tell you what procurement route they wish to follow and the contract form to use.

You must be aware of these contract forms, and know when it might be appropriate for you to recommend their use to your clients. Have an understanding of these forms and discuss their relative merits with your clients when their use is being considered.

If your client requires you to use one of these forms, make sure you understand fully the contract requirements and your changed role and responsibilities.

■ **Design and Build Contract (DB)**

This is appropriate where the contractor is to complete the design and where the employer employs an agent (either in-house or consultant) to administer the contract conditions.

The problem for architects with design–build contracts is the variety of ways in which this procurement route can be used. If design–build appears to be the most appropriate procurement route, the decision to use it needs to be taken if possible when agreeing the client's brief (Section 3, page 43) as it will probably have a profound effect on how you manage your work and on your subsequent role and responsibilities, particularly if you are novated to the contractor by your client.

Potential problem areas with design–build are explored in Sections 2, 3 and 5.

■ **Management Building Contract (MC)**

This form is used for large-scale projects requiring an early start on site, where the works are designed by the employer's design team and where it is not possible to complete full design information before work commences on site. The contractor merely manages the contract, employing works contractors to carry out the construction.

It is best to let the quantity surveyor recommend the use of this contract to your client, for while it has advantages, the client will not know the final cost until after completion – when it will be too late to do anything about it!

In *Construction Management*, first published by JCT in January 2002, the two separate contract management methods are described as:

Management contracting where the client enters into separate contracts with a designer and a management contractor who then enters into sub-contracts with works contractors.

Construction management is where the client enters into separate contracts with the designer, a construction manager and with each separate works contractor.

Management contracts have been known to go horribly wrong, which is one reason why they are not in such wide use now as at one time. Only very expe-

rienced, sophisticated and well-organised clients should use the construction management method.

- **Major Project Construction Contract (MP)**

This form is intended for large projects and where the employer regularly procures large-scale construction work. Architects are more likely to be told to use this contract by their clients rather than advise them on its use.

If your client chooses to use this procurement route, make sure you understand your role as the architect and the way the contract is intended to work.

- **Prime Cost Building Contract (PCC)**

This form is for 'projects requiring an early start on site and where full design information is not available before the work commences'. Dangerous words! If you recommend the use of this contract to your client, make sure they understand this is a time cost plus contract and that the final cost is not known until after completion.

The problem is that starting any contract before your detail design is complete creates the need to ensure the construction information is delivered to the contractor when required, not necessarily when that item of work is due to start on site.

You must make sure you can deliver construction information when required by the contractor. Otherwise, you will have problems.

- **Measured Term Contract (MTC)**

This form is useful where an employer has a regular flow of maintenance and minor work to be carried out by a single contractor over a specified period of time and under a single contract. As the work is measured and valued after completion against an agreed schedule of rates, the final cost is not known until after that item of work has been completed.

Recommend its use in those circumstances and no other!

- **Framework Agreement (FA)**

This contract is for procurement of building work over a period of time, where the parties are legally bound by the provisions of the framework agreement used in conjunction with the contract form. It is effectively a partnership agreement. Your client will almost certainly tell you that they have decided to enter into this contract rather than ask you to advise on its use.

You may be asked to sign a framework agreement with a client. It offers the possibility of a continuity of new work, but do be clear as to the responsibilities you will be entering into as this will be a legally binding agreement on you as well as the client.

If you are required to act as architect when the client is proposing to use this form of agreement, either with you or with contractors, do make sure you fully understand your role and responsibilities before you accept the appointment.

- **Framework Agreement Guide (FA/G)**

Framework agreements in this form are relatively new and are invariably used by sophisticated clients who have a continuing programme of work and wish to make long-term agreements with contractors for an advance programme of work. If you have clients in this position and they require you to work under these arrangements, do read and understand this guide. It takes a practical approach to completing the contract, advising on unfamiliar terms and specifying roles and responsibilities for completion.

Existing projects

Many projects will continue to operate under the pre-2011 JCT contracts so you will need to keep up to speed on those forms for some years.

However, because the JCT 2011 contracts are based on changes to legislation it is not advisable to start new projects on pre-2011 JCT contracts.

Use the appropriate JCT forms and ensure you understand all the supporting documents that are available.

Tender documents

Contractors base their tenders for work on the tender documents you prepare. These documents must be accurate in describing the building you have designed and how you wish them to be translated into the completed building. Any omissions or contradictions will lead to problems, which will be down to you to resolve. If the errors in the tender documents increase the cost or cause delay, you will have to explain why to your client. At best they will not be impressed; at worst they may have a claim against you.

Insufficient time to prepare comprehensive tender documents usually means the contract starts on site with incomplete construction information. This then results in information being provided late to the contractor, leading to claims for delay and disruption.

Ensure that you, and any other consultants employed by the client, have sufficient time in which to prepare the necessary drawings, details, specifications and bills of quantities on which tenders will be based. The more detailed and accurate the tender information, the better the contractors' tenders will reflect the final cost of what is actually going to be built.

If your client denies you the necessary time to prepare complete tender documents, ensure they are aware of the possible consequences, and that while you will do your best, they carry the risks involved – not you!

Check all tender documents carefully before issue. Incomplete or incorrect tender documents will cause problems for you and your client later. Cutting corners now may save time, but it usually leads to extra costs. Your client must be aware of this and understand the risks involved.

So, double-check all documents before they are issued.

- Is all the information being provided correct and is it up to date?
- Have you clearly set out all the information you will require from the contractors with the submission of their tender?
- Are all the client's design, construction, phasing and completion requirements included clearly and unambiguously in the documents?

While you may not be competent to check other consultants' specialist design in detail, check with them that they have included all the information required by the contractor for tender purposes. Also, make sure they have checked their tender documents and drawings for accuracy and completeness.

The main provisions to be covered in the contract documents will have been discussed and agreed at earlier stages. All important items will have been referred to in the contractors' 'invitation to tender' documents. If a quantity surveyor has prepared bills of quantities, the form of contract to be used and any specific requirements should be covered in the bills' preambles.

Avoid if possible altering standard form clauses or adding additional ad hoc clauses unless absolutely necessary. If changes to standard forms are requested by your client, get them to agree with their lawyers the precise wording to be included and that they fully appreciate the implications of the changes.

Check carefully when the first copy of the bill of quantities is sent to you by the quantity surveyor that everything agreed on the contract provisions has been fully covered and that there are no errors or omissions.

Design–build situations

Be particularly careful with design–build contracts where you are acting for the design–build contractor and working up another architect's designs or client's sketches. The employer's requirements will be the client's brief to the contractor. Check them carefully to ensure they are complete and that what is described or shown on drawings will work. If the requirements are not complete, it is your duty to warn your client, the design–build contractor, of any discrepancies or omissions.

Design–build contractors have to submit the contractor's proposals as part of their bid. If, in the hurry to get the bid in and to keep costs down, instead of preparing your own drawings you merely copy those in the employer's requirements without properly checking them, it can lead to serious problems later.

Recommending contractors

You may wish to, or be asked by the client to, recommend suitable contractors to invite to tender. Before doing so, check on the suitability and financial strength of all contractors. This applies also to key sub-contractors and suppliers who you (or the client) may wish to nominate for specialist work.

There will be a high cost in time and money to your client should the contractor go bankrupt during progress of the contract, or if the quality of the contractor's work or progress is such that the client decides to terminate the contract. If you cannot show that you carried out all reasonable checks before recommending them, your client will have a complaint, if not a claim!

Before recommending contractors to clients, check their performance record and financial stability. Should there be problems later, you must be able to show that you took all reasonable precautions to avoid your client being landed with these problems.

Provisional sums

If time is short it is tempting to cover large items of work, which cannot be fully designed, detailed, specified and billed at tender stage, with the catch-all label: 'provisional sums'. This is dangerous. Only include provisional sums when there is no reasonable alternative. The details will have to be settled later, when it may cause delays with the information flow to the contractor, leading to claims that will increase the final cost to the client.

Late construction information to the contractor is a gift to their claims depart-ment! Once the contract has started on site, you are playing catch-up.

Contractor-designed portions

Another short cut at tender stage when there is no time to detail parts of the building is to make these 'contractor-designed' items. Used properly, this is a perfectly acceptable way to deal with parts of the building where specialised design is required and is best made a contractor's responsibility.

However, when used merely as a means of shifting detail design responsibility for work that should properly be designed by you, it can lead to extra costs and problems during construction.

Only use the contractor-design option when it is the best way to deal with that part of the design of your building. Do not use it because you do not have the time or capacity to design it yourself.

Building insurances

Existing and new buildings under construction must be insured. Third party risks, damage to adjoining buildings and personal injury have to be covered. Standard forms of contract set out the risks to be covered and who is to insure. Do ensure that you are aware of insurance requirements in the suite of JCT contracts. If dealing with the major projects form (MP), a considerable amount of pre-contract effort has to be invested in getting the insurance arrangements correct.

So, who insures what, and for how long?

With new buildings, the contractor will almost certainly be required to take out all of the insurances and indemnify the client against all claims during construction. With alterations to existing buildings, where, for example, a fire can cause extensive damage during the building work, the client is normally required to insure the existing property and the works in joint names. This may prove to be a problem if the client does not control the building insurance – being a tenant where the landlord insures, for example. The situation will be even more complicated if the building being altered is in partial occupation. There are a lot of potential tripwires in this area.

You, as the architect, have a responsibility to ensure that the insurances required under the building contract are in place and comply with contract requirements. You may be held liable if the required insurance cover is not in place should disaster strike. However, as an architect, you are not an expert on insurance. Do not hold yourself out to have that expertise.

"The crucial issue is never to advise clients on areas outside your expertise as an architect. Remember, you are not an expert on insurance."

Ask the client to arrange for their insurance broker's advice on the insurances required to protect them from all risks while the building work is carried out. When the contract is to be placed, arrange for their brokers to check that the insurances as required by the contract to be taken out by the client or contractor are in place and cover the required specified risks. Ensure your client asks their broker if there are any other risks that the client should cover. For example, business interruption if damage causes a delay in completion.

Also advise your client to arrange for their broker to make whatever periodic checks are necessary to ensure the policies as required by the contract are in force for the whole of the requisite contract period. The policies will almost certainly be annual policies taken out by the contractor. It is important to ensure they are renewed on time and with the necessary cover. This is particularly important with smaller contractors, but even the big boys have been known to get into difficulties with their insurances.

If your client does not have a broker who specialises in this type of insurance, ask them to arrange for a specialist broker to be available to check the documents. If they refuse, you will be wise to employ your own specialist broker. It may cost a small fee, but it is your insurance policy against the worst case scenario. Existing buildings being converted have been known to be set on fire through the sub-contractor's negligence. If the necessary insurance is not in place, you may have a disaster situation on your hands.

Be careful if the client is taking part possession of the site before completion of the whole contract. If this has been envisaged in the original contract arrangements, the insurances required to cover the parts taken over by the client and those still being worked on by the contractor should have been arranged. It will be important to ensure they are in place and complied with.

If partial occupation takes place outside of the provisions of the signed contract, possibly as a result of delays in completing the contract, it will probably be necessary to make special insurance provisions. Again, this is a matter for insurance brokers to decide – not the architect. You must, however, draw your client's attention to the need for them to deal with what may be complicated insurance requirements.

The crucial issue is never to advise clients on areas outside your expertise as an architect. Remember, you are not an expert on insurance.

Completion date

Does the client require you to specify in the tender documents a time for completion, or is it to be left to the contractor to submit the construction time (which will become a key contract requirement) with their tender?

If you specify a completion date, the tender will reflect this rather than the time the contractor considers will be required to complete. If you leave it to the contractor to specify in their tender how long it will take to build, your client may be faced with a difficult decision – lower cost or earlier completion.

Will time be of the essence for the contract?

If so, you must specify the completion date the contractor has to achieve. Make it clear to the contractor that time will be of the essence. Make sure the client understands that this will make it all the more important for sufficient time to be allocated for the design process and that client changes during construction will put the completion date under threat.

Liquidated damages for late completion

Agree the level of liquidated damages that will be included in the contract. These must be no more than the estimated financial loss to the client if completion is delayed beyond the contract period. They must not be a penalty. Consult the client as to the amount of liquidated damages to be included, based on their estimated losses. Confirm this to the client in writing and keep a note of how the damages figure was arrived at in case it is ever questioned.

Staged completion

Have you correctly interpreted the client's requirements as to staged or sequential completion? What are the complications with building insurance? Who covers what when the client or their fitting-out contractors move in?

Make sure these issues are fully covered in the contract you recommend to your client.

Statutory requirements

Check that the contract documents will be compliant with the Construction Act's requirements on:

- 'pay when paid' clauses
- 'pay when certified' clauses
- the right to suspend some or all work obligations for late or non-payment
- adjudication provisions.

Naming the adjudicator

Decide whether an adjudicator is to be named in the contract or if the choice of adjudicator is to be left until a dispute arises.

As adjudication is a short notice and quick decision process, it is probably best to nominate one of the professional bodies to appoint an adjudicator when a dispute arises. (Details of the RIBA Adjudication Service are available from the RIBA Practice Department.) If you name a person in the contract, they may not be immediately available or not have the specialist experience to deal with that specific matter.

Health and safety regulations

The tender documents should cover the duties of the contractor regarding compliance with all relevant health and safety regulations. The name of the CDM co-ordinator to be appointed by the client should be stated.

Possession of the *entire* site?

Are you sure the client can make the whole of the site available to the contractor on the date stated in the tender documents? Check again the site availability with the client just before you go to tender and again just before you ask them to sign the building contract.

Start-up time

Give contractors sufficient time to prepare their tenders. If you ask for too much too soon you will get either faulty or unnecessarily high tenders. Either way, you will have problems.

Be satisfied that the time specified between the acceptance of the tender by the client and the date on which the contractor will start on site is sufficient time for you to provide them with all the information they need to start. Also, be sure that you can provide the contractor with the further design and construction information (and that of the other consultants) when they are required. Late information will lead to claims for delay and disruption, for which your client may hold you responsible.

Finally, do not rely on the quantity surveyor or the project manager to deal with these very important contract matters. You, as the architect and ultimately the contract administrator, have the final responsibility for co-ordinating the work of the other consultants and for the completeness and accuracy of the contract documents.

If you allow work to start on site too soon, everyone involved will be chasing their tails in no time at all!

Preparing the contract documents

Be clear who is to be responsible for preparing the contract documents for signature by your client and the contractor.

Whichever contract form is chosen, if you are responsible for preparing the contract documents you must ensure all the agreed details, changes, omissions or additional clauses are included. Ensure optional clauses are left in or crossed out, and that liquidated damages and partial or sequential completion and insurance requirements tally exactly with the equivalent tender clauses.

If the quantity surveyor is responsible for preparing the contract documents, ensure they are checked by you to confirm they are complete and as agreed before they are signed.

The successful tenderer has offered to construct your building on the basis of your tender documents. Any variation between the tender documents and the contract documents, which bind your client and the contractor in a legal agreement, will create problems and potential claims by the contractor against your client. Your client may then try to recover their costs against you as the party being responsible for the contractual problems that the mistake has created.

So, check carefully that the contract documents correctly reflect the accepted tender documents, with no errors, omissions or contradictions. Check with the other consultants and make sure they confirm the contract documents reflect accurately their requirements and what was included in the tender documents covering their work.

Ideally, you should have all the documents attached to the contract, stamped and initialled by both parties as 'the contract document referred to in the contract dated . . . , etc.'. If this is not practical due to the number of documents involved, a list must be attached to the contract. Be careful that the drawing numbers listed include the revisions on which the contract is based and are clearly identified as such. Trying to establish later which was the correct revision can cause problems.

Check and double-check final contract documents. Then get your partner, project architect or even the quantity surveyor to check again, just to be quite sure!

Client awareness

Before asking the client to sign the contract documents, attach an 'executive summary' of the obligations of both the client and the contractor. It is important that clients, particularly 'lay' clients additionally protected by consumer law, are fully aware of their obligations in the contract you are recommending them to sign.

Emphasise the variation clauses and the need to avoid client changes during construction, stressing cost and delay implications. Diplomatically explain your role and authority as architect in the contract, where at times you are obliged to act impartially between client and contractor. These are decisions that you have to make which the client may not like, particularly as they are paying your fees!

Make it clear to the client that if they give instructions directly to the contractor or workers on site, your control over the contract on costs and time will be made very difficult, if not impossible. As frustrating as it may be for them, all instructions must be passed through you. Explain that this is in their interests and that you will accept no responsibility for extra costs or delays caused by their giving direct instructions.

Explain the adjudication procedures for dealing with disputes during construction. As the contractor is more likely than the client to invoke those, it is as well that the clients know up-front rather than being surprised when it happens.

Ensure the client understands that it is your responsibility to inspect the work in progress in order to check it is being carried out in accordance with the contract, but it is not your job to supervise the contractor.

If you are asked to place an architect on site full-time, ensure their day-to-day responsibilities are agreed in advance: whether they are there to provide constant supervision or just to make on-the-spot decisions on design matters that are your responsibility. Also, make sure that you are properly recompensed, not only for their time costs but also the additional day-to-day responsibility you have accepted.

Ensure the client has a signed and completed contract form and all supporting documents and that they understand the obligations on them in the contract you have got them to sign.

Avoid changes

Discourage your client from making changes during construction. Warn them in writing of any cost and time consequences. Equally, you cannot afford the luxury of second thoughts on design at this stage unless unavoidable. If you do so and it results in claims for extra costs and delays, you will have difficulty justifying these to your client.

If you discover design or specification errors during construction that require rectification, you must instruct the necessary changes. Explain the problem to your client at the time, not at the end of the contract.

"Contractors see any change as increasing the cost, so do all you can to avoid changes."

Contractors see any change as increasing the cost, so do all you can to avoid changes.

Payments to the contractor

Set out for the client the arrangements for the issue of certificates, the requirement for them to be paid on time and the penalties for not doing so. If possible, give the client an updated approximate cash-flow forecast so they will know how much they will be expected to pay and when. You or the quantity surveyor should have given them indicative cash-flow forecasts from the earliest stage when some idea of time and cost could be forecast.

Check contract documents against the contractor's tender

When sending the contract documents to the contractor for signature, put the obligation on them to check the documents against their tender and confirm there are no errors or omissions in relation to their accepted tender, including all agreed post-tender changes, before they sign the contract.

Agreed changes to the contractor's tender not reflected in the final contract documents lead to complications you can well do without!

Starting work on site

Get to this stage and everyone involved will want to get on with the job without delay. Be careful. Many contracts are started before the final contract documents are agreed, let alone signed – a situation that can lead to disputes later. Resist starting before contracts are signed, but if it is unavoidable your client must be aware of the reasons and the risks.

If your client is pressing you to commence the building work, ensure they are aware of the implications of work starting without a signed contract. Is the client prepared to accept the risks involved? Warn them in writing of the risks so that they make the decision to start knowing all the facts.

Do all you can to get three copies of the contract documents prepared, agreed and signed before any work is started on site and to ensure one completed copy is given to the client. Instil the discipline not to allow contract signing to drift on unchecked.

Get the contract signed!

Absurd as it may seem, there are frequent cases where architects have indicated to their clients which contract form would be used, but have never prepared the documents or have not got them signed by the client or the contractor! You must prepare a suitable form of contract for all but the smallest and simplest of contracts and get them signed by both parties, preferably before work starts on site, and you must have provided a copy to the client.

Letters of intent

Unless there are inescapable reasons for starting work on site before contracts have been finalised, advise your clients very strongly against issuing 'letters of intent'. However well-drafted they may be, if a problem arises these documents soon become meat for lawyers, who may dispute their precise meaning and what should be paid if formal contract documents are not subsequently signed.

You and your clients can do without these expensive legal arguments. In almost all cases, given the will the contract can be finalised and signed before a start on site is authorised. If a premature start is unavoidable, it is better to agree a limited package of initial work within defined limits and an agreed cost with no commitment to continue if for whatever reason the contract does not proceed.

Advise your clients against issuing letters of intent. If they must, insist the letters are drafted by their lawyers and not by you!

Contract management

Sloppy contract management by architects results in contractors' claims for extra costs, delays and extensions of time. So set up clear office procedures for the management of all your contracts. At the outset of each specific contract adjust your standardised procedures as necessary to suit that contract and incorporate any lessons learned from earlier contract problems.

Your responsibilities

Be clear as to the extent and limits of your responsibilities and authority and those of the other parties involved in the contract. Avoid making decisions that should be made by others – you may be taking on liabilities which are not yours and for which you may not be insured.

Project managers

Where a project manager is appointed by the client, make sure (as set out in Section 3) that the respective roles and responsibilities of you, the architect, and the project manager are clearly set out by the client, and that they are understood by all parties. The project manager's responsibilities can overrule the architect's in certain areas, but cannot change the architect's role and responsibility as the contract administrator appointed to administer the contract.

Contractor's programme

The contractor is obliged to provide you with their contract work programme. You need a detailed programme, preferably more than a simple bar chart, to be able to deal with any claims by the contractor for disruption and delay.

A critical path analysis identifying the key operations or stages crucial to completion on time is the best form of programme. Realistically, however much you try, contractors are rarely prepared to provide such a programme, at least not until after the contract is completed, when they are attempting to substantiate claims for delays and extensions of time. If you can obtain one, contractors are usually reluctant to provide architects with the degree of detail you will require to monitor the contract work on site as it proceeds.

If possible, draft your own critical path analysis to establish the dates of the key work operations or material supply that will delay the contract if they are not achieved. The earlier you do this, the better.

One way to achieve a detailed contractor's programme, with critical path operations identified, is to do this when you are agreeing the schedule of dates by which outstanding design and construction information is to be provided by you. At that stage, the contractor will be anxious to impress on you the dates by which you must provide information that is critical to progress and completion. Spend time with the contractor at the start of the contract, going through their programme and identifying key operations for which commencement or completion will be critical to keeping the project on time.

On your site visits, monitor and record actual progress against the contractor's programme. If there are delays, try to get the contractor to agree and record actual delay at regular intervals. If you have prepared your own critical path programme, check it constantly against your programme to see how it is affected by actual progress. You will need all this information later, probably after practical completion, when you have to deal with any contractor's claims for disruption and delays and claims for extensions of time.

It can be very useful for you to ask the contractor at an early stage for their projection of expenditure (their construction spend) based on their programme. It can be a very good guide, not only for giving your client advance notice of likely payments, but also for checking if the contractor is falling behind programme. It can also be useful evidence when dealing with claims for extension of time.

Information supply

Be totally objective as to further information in the way of drawings or decisions the contractor will need to enable them to carry out the contract efficiently and without delays. You must ensure the contractor cannot claim extra costs because of late information from you. Prepare a schedule of information required; agree dates, based on the contractor's programme, for delivery of information to the contractor during construction. You must then ensure you keep to those agreed information flow dates.

As you have the responsibility of co-ordinating the work of your client's other consultants in the contract, check that they have agreed with the contractor similar information provision schedules and that they are adhering to them.

If you are under pressure to provide construction information by the agreed time, avoid the temptation to assume that you can provide your information later than agreed because the contractor is behind programme. They are entitled to the information by a reasonable date before the work it covers has to be carried out on site. If you provide your design information later than the date originally agreed, the contractor will use this to claim they were disrupted and delayed because of your late information.

If you have provided the information by the date you agreed with the contractor, there can be no such claim.

Accurate records

Have a system for accurately recording the date and nature of all information you send out so that at any time in the future there can be no arguments. In particular, record specifically the latest amendments. This applies particularly to drawings re-issued with new amendments. Sloppy records make it difficult to refute contract claims and severely damage your defence against a negligence claim!

Keeping accurate records may take time but is always worth the effort.

Rapid information transfer systems

Use, where appropriate, rapid information transfer systems (fax, e-mail and the internet) between your office and site to resolve issues as they arise. Ensure the system sends copies to the contractor's office and to all others who should be kept informed.

Keep permanent dated records of all such information. When using the telephone, keep an accurate dated record of the conversation on file. Make sure it is mirrored correctly in any confirmation in writing. Remember if you are still using fax that some forms of fax paper fade within months! So have a hard copy of the fax. Sent or received.

Do be very careful with the wording of internal notes, e-mails or memos. If the contract becomes the subject of legal proceedings, all documents have to be disclosed to the other side. A sloppy internal note saying 'what a mess we are in', when discovered later by the other side, does not help your case. *This is known as 'whoopee' evidence by the other side.*

Architect's instructions

Make it clear to the contractor that only your instructions confirmed in writing will be accepted as evidence to support any claims for extra costs or extensions of time. But make sure you confirm your instructions in writing and state whether they constitute an 'extra'.

Set up clear procedures with the contractor for dealing with the architect's instructions. Do not leave it to the contractor to confirm back to you what they consider to be 'architect's instructions'. You give the instructions and confirm them in writing on site or immediately on your return to the office.

If possible, avoid giving instructions for work that will increase costs until you have either a quantity surveyor's estimate or, even better, agreed the extra cost with the contractor. Confirm all architect's instructions in writing.

Cost control

A contract has a contract cost. The client expects this to be the maximum amount of money they will have to pay for the building. Many will still think this even when they know they have made changes. Even if they accept they caused the extra cost, they often say 'there is no way I thought it would cost as much as that!'

You must, therefore, institute a tight and regular cost-control system at the start of the contract and maintain it right through to completion. Monitor regularly how variations will affect final cost. Keep your client informed of the cost of significant 'extras'. If possible, obtain the client's agreement to all significant extras as they arise to avoid giving them nasty surprises later.

Have a periodic 'final cost' update no less frequently than monthly. If you have a quantity surveyor, they can be instructed to constantly monitor costs and make regular reports. Without a quantity surveyor you must discipline yourself to keep abreast at all times of significant cost changes and prepare your own final cost assessment at least once a month.

Assess the cost of client changes immediately they are known. Agree the extra cost involved with the contractor and, if possible, obtain your client's agreement to the extra cost before the work is carried out. If that is not possible, notify the client of the extra cost as soon as it is known and how it will affect the final cost.

Clients do not like surprises – particularly cost overruns!

Notices under the contract

Have a checklist of the content and timing of notices to be given by you, or to be received from the contractor, under the contract to ensure you do not find yourself in trouble because you did not follow the requirements of the contract. Make sure the wording of notices is correct and that they are given within the time limits specified in the contract.

Ensure that all notices required for contracts covered by the Construction Act as amended are complied with and frequently check that the systems you have set up are being operated consistently and correctly in your office. You may think they are, but unless you check you cannot be sure.

Site visits and inspections

Site visits are not just meetings to discuss progress and problem solving. When on site, your prime responsibility is to inspect the work in progress to check it complies with the contract. Make sure you have sufficient time to inspect work in progress as well as to sit in site huts in site meetings agreeing minutes!

Never hold yourself out to be 'supervising'. Your responsibility is to periodically inspect the work in progress on site to ensure as far as possible that it is in accordance with the contract. You are not supervising but inspecting the progress of the contract.

Be on site to inspect important items of work and at specific stages, particularly just before you issue a certificate. Time your visits so that you are on site when vital areas of work are being carried out, rather than just at regular pre-arranged intervals. The occasional ad hoc unannounced site visit can also be useful for keeping people on their toes.

How frequently you visit the site will depend on the size, complexity and timing of the contract as well as your appointment contract. For large, long-running contracts, if a clerk of works has been appointed, monthly visits may be sufficient. In most cases, fortnightly will be more appropriate. In the case of a very intensive, short-period contract, such as a shop fit-out, daily visits may be warranted.

Do not be tempted to reduce the number of site inspections because your internal cost-control system indicates you have spent all the fees allocated to contract administration of that job. If you reduce the number of site visits below what is necessary, your financial loss may be greater because you have not carried out your inspection duties properly and breaches of the contract have passed by without challenge from you. You will then be in even bigger trouble!

Day-to-day supervision

If the client requires or you advise that day-to-day inspection of work in progress is necessary, then a clerk of works should be appointed and paid by the client. You should be involved in interviewing candidates and be comfortable with whoever is appointed as they will work under your control.

This can be a significant increase in your responsibilities and legal liabilities, so the clerk of works must be selected carefully and you need to be satisfied they are carrying out their duties diligently. Their competence will be, at least to a degree, your responsibility.

Clients' representatives

Some clients wish to appoint their own site representative. In these circumstances it is essential their authority on site, and particularly how this may impinge on your role and responsibilities as the contract administrator, is spelt out clearly and understood by all involved in advance and confirmed in writing. It is also essential that all instructions they wish to give to the contractor must be through you and not direct. If there is any serious erosion of your responsibilities, as set out in the contract, you should withdraw from those duties immediately.

Progress recording

Keep written and photographic records of progress. Many contract disputes relate to what had been built at a particular time. Modern digital cameras enable you to take your own dated photographs, which can be invaluable evidence later as to progress achieved by a certain date. On larger contracts, you can require the contractor to commission regular site progress photographs, which they may do anyway. The more detailed records you have as to what had been built by a recorded date, the better you will be able to deal with any contractor's claims and client's complaints.

Extensions of time

If the building contract contains clauses allowing the client to deduct damages for late completion, the contractor can claim an extension of time to the completion date in the contract if, in general terms, they have not caused the delay.

Granting a fair and reasonable extension of time is important to both contractor and client. The contractor will claim the maximum extension of time they feel they can justify because it protects them from having late completion damages deducted from their certificates. If you grant a greater extension than is justified, you deprive your client of the opportunity to deduct the damages for late completion to which they are entitled, which will probably be a considerable sum of money.

Claims for extension of time are invariably complex and it is difficult to make decisions that both sides will consider to be fair and reasonable.

Avoiding extension of time claims

The best way to avoid extension of time claims is to ensure that if the contract is delayed, the cause of the delay is the contractor's responsibility under the contract and not yours or the client's. So, do the following.

- Make sure the whole of the contract site is available when required in the contract.
- Make sure that as far as possible the building is sufficiently designed and detailed before you start on site.

- Make sure that all outstanding construction information is provided to the contractor by the dates agreed and not when you think they need it on site. The contractor will argue that they needed that information much earlier to order the materials and plan the work involved in carrying out your instructions.
- Dissuade your client from making changes to what is in the contract documents. Any deviation from the contract gives the contractor the opportunity to claim disruption to their work and delay to the contract.
- Above all, avoid changing your mind. Refining your design when the building is under construction may produce a better building but, unless absolutely essential, will almost certainly lead to a claim for extra costs and probably an extension of time.

If you and your client follow that advice you should reduce your exposure to extension of time claims dramatically although not completely.

Contractors' claims for extensions of time

The contractor is required, forthwith, to give you written notice whenever it becomes reasonably apparent that the progress of the works is being or is likely to be delayed. This applies whether or not completion is likely to be delayed.

On receipt of a contractor's claim, check your duties and the procedures to be followed against the contract documents. First, you have to decide whether the delay has been caused by a 'relevant event'. It is important not to grant an extension of time if the cause of the delay is not a relevant event as set out in the contract.

Relevant events are listed in clause 2.29 of the JCT 11 Standard Building Contract (SBC). Some examples of relevant events include the following:

- Force majeure – basically, circumstances that are 'acts of God' or are beyond the power of the contractor to control.
- Exceptionally adverse weather conditions. Note the word 'exceptionally' – heavy rain showers in April or normal falls of snow in January are not examples of exceptional weather conditions. The contractor should have anticipated that weather when tendering and preparing their work programmes.
- Loss or damage caused by specified perils. These are defined in clause 6.8 of JCT 11 and include fire, explosion, storm, overflowing of water tanks, riots, civil commotion or strikes, but exclude expected risks.

Next, you have to judge whether the delay caused by the relevant event is likely to cause the completion of the contract to be delayed, not whether present or future progress is or will be delayed.

You are required to reply to the contractor within 12 weeks of receipt of all the information you reasonably require from the contractor to come to a decision about whether an extension of time is warranted, and, if so, how much.

Within 12 weeks after the date of practical completion, you are obliged to review any extensions of time already granted, taking into account what actually happened on site with regard to delays and any relevant events that you are aware of, even if the contractor has not notified them. If you consider it fair and reasonable, you must grant further extensions of time.

Do not come to a decision until you are satisfied that you have sufficient information available to you in order for you to make a fair and reasonable assessment of any claim for an extension of time.

Contractor's programmes and your own records of actual progress of the work against programmes will be important factors in your coming to a decision as to whether a further extension of time is justified, and if so, how much. If you developed a critical path analysis programme with the contractor, it will be invaluable to help you establish whether the delaying event has caused the completion of the contract to be delayed.

Assessing extensions of time is not an exact science; it is your judgement based on the facts available to you at the time. Providing you have done all that was reasonably possible to assemble all relevant information, and you can demonstrate that you have been fair and reasonable to both parties in arriving at your decision, you are unlikely to be challenged by arbitration or in the courts, unless very large sums of money are involved.

Interim certificates

You are responsible for issuing interim certificates. If the client employs a quantity surveyor, it will be their responsibility to check and agree the contractor's valuation of work in progress based on instructions from you. However, you sign and issue the certificate. The amount certified and paid is in the end your responsibility. So, if you have any doubts about the value and what is included, raise them with the quantity surveyor and make any corrections before issuing the certificate.

The procedure for the issue of interim certificates has become more stringent under JCT 11. You are required to issue the interim certificate within five days of the payment due date, otherwise a default notice may be issued by the contractor. This notice will become payable unless a payless notice is issued by the employer. To avoid the circumstance of notices and counter notices, it is recommended that you issue the required interim certificates on time.

It is your responsibility to ensure the contractor is not overpaid. While an overpayment may be corrected in later certificates, should the contractor go bust before completion or the contract is terminated, your client will have lost money by overpayment and you will almost certainly have a claim for negligence to deal with.

Exclude defective work

Ensure that defective work that is not acceptable to you under the terms of the contract is not included in the valuation. Check with other consultants before agreeing the valuation for a certificate that all of the work for which they are responsible meets the contract requirements. The onus is on you to tell the quantity surveyor what is not acceptable and must be excluded when they prepare the valuation for the certificate.

If defective work is included, it is not normally a major problem, provided the defects are remedied before practical completion. However, should the contractor go bust or the contract be terminated before the defective work is remedied, you could have major problems to deal with.

Off-site fittings

Be very careful when including the value of prefabricated items or fittings being manufactured off site. Ideally, do not include them until they are on site and fixed. For large items with long manufacturing times this may not be realistic, so visit where they are being manufactured to ensure they have reached the stage and value claimed. Ensure they are clearly defined in the certificate valuation so if there are problems later with ownership there is proof they have been paid for!

Valuations

If there is no quantity surveyor, you are on your own. The onus is on you to check and agree the contractor's valuations for interim certificates. In that case, you should have a priced specification or schedule of work from which you can check the work items that have been completed to your satisfaction. Where you have to make a guess at the value of partially completed work, err on the safe side in the amount you include. Keep a record of how you arrive at the amount you certify.

When problems arise, the amount of money you have certified to be paid to the contractor invariably comes under acute examination.

Practical completion certificates

Practical completion certificates present special problems. Contractors want them issued as soon as possible as this will release half of their money that has been retained in interim certificates. It also releases them from other obligations, such as insurance and site security, and triggers the contractor's defects liability period.

Importantly for both parties, it also prevents any further deduction of liquidated damages for non-completion on time. However, the client may want to delay issue until they are ready to take up occupation and continue to deduct liquidated damages. It is your responsibility to issue this certificate and you must act impartially between your client and the contractor.

If there are only minor outstanding defective or incomplete items of work, discuss these with your client and obtain their agreement to the certificate being issued. There are no absolute rules. Decide each situation on its merits, based on the contract wording that the building has to be 'practically' but not absolutely complete.

If the client takes occupation of the whole building it will almost certainly be deemed practical completion. It will be difficult to argue that practical completion has not been achieved.

If there are any reasons for which the contractor is responsible that prevent the building being occupied, or there is more than a *minimal* amount of outstanding work (which must include remedy of defective work), you should not issue the practical completion certificate. Although outstanding items may be minor, if there is a significant number of them it would entail significant disruption to the client for them to be completed or rectified when the building is occupied – this gives sufficient reason to refuse to issue a practical completion certificate.

If your client agrees to the issue of the practical completion certificate even though there are significant items of work still outstanding or to be rectified, attach a schedule of outstanding or defective items to the certificate and specify when and how this work is to be carried out.

If you have reasonable doubts about issuing the practical completion certificate, issue instead a further interim certificate valuing all completed work, with a schedule of outstanding items to be completed to your satisfaction before you can certify practical completion. This will not only protect your position but will also give the contractor the incentive to complete all outstanding items – they will want to get their practical completion certificate as soon as possible.

Rectification or defects liability period

Within the designated rectification period in JCT 11, inspect the building and prepare and serve on the contractor a schedule of the defects that are the contractor's responsibility. Remember, this is a 'rectification' period, not an opportunity for your client to have normal maintenance items or wear and tear as a result of the building being occupied repaired at the contractor's expense.

Make sure the schedule is served before the rectification period expires otherwise it may be repudiated by the contractor. Then pressurise the contractor to complete the work without undue delay. This does not normally figure high on a contractor's priority list unless they are desperate for the cash that will be released with the final certificate. The longer it drifts on, the more it will cost you in time chasing for it to be completed. You will not get any extra fees from your client, so it is in your interest not to allow it to drift on.

Final accounts

You cannot issue the final certificate until you or the quantity surveyor agree the final contract cost. Agreement of the final account tends to drift on, usually because everyone is either too busy with other more profitable or pressing work or arguing over claims.

Get the final account settled as soon as possible. It is the cause of irritation for all involved if it is allowed to drift and is not dealt with expeditiously. If you have settled contractor's claims as you went along, agreeing the final account should not be difficult.

If there is a large, complicated claims situation, try to achieve agreement to a broad figure settlement as soon as possible. The cost to your client and you of prolonged arguments, particularly if lawyers are involved, cannot be controlled and may eventually be more than the amount in dispute.

Contractors always claim for more than they expect to get. Clients say they will not pay more than a certain amount, but in the end will usually pay more to settle. So, try to establish how much divides them and, if possible, advise a settlement that avoids big legal bills. Collected evidence indicates that virtually all contractor claims are eventually settled, either by negotiation, arbitration or in the courts, at between 30 and 35 per cent of the original claim.

Go through the contractor's final account with your client to ensure they understand how the final cost is reached. Point out the extras that result from client changes and explain those which do not. If you have kept your client fully informed of all major cost variations during progress, you should not give them any major surprises.

In the end, however, you may have to decide with the help of the quantity surveyor (if there is one) the final cost you consider impartially to be the fair and reasonable amount the contractor is due. But in case you have to justify this later, make sure that both sides, including your client, have been consulted and that you made your decision based on all the facts and in accordance with the contract conditions.

Final certificates

You can only issue the final certificate when the final cost has been agreed with the contractor, or failing that when you have established (acting impartially) what you consider to be the final amount due to the contractor.

Be absolutely sure before you issue the final certificate that:

- your client is not aware of any outstanding matters that require attention
- all known defects have been rectified
- no new defects have emerged since you carried out your last inspection
- the contractor has met all their obligations under the contract.

JCT 11 makes it clear that the issue of a final certificate does not release the contractor from liability for latent defects with materials and workmanship.

Having issued the final certificate, your duties under the contract end. Pack up the files, title them clearly and place them in your dead file storage. Keep the files for least 15 years, just in case.

See also:
Civil law
claims, page
101

SUMMARY

- Ensure that your tender documents include all the information contractors require in order to submit accurate prices for the work. This will also ensure there are no contradictions that could lead to misunderstandings and later arguments as to what was, or was not, included.
- Specify the standard form of contract to be used, including optional and other clauses. Emphasise any special requirements, such as 'time is of the essence'.
- Use the JCT 11 contract forms, and ensure you understand and use the integrated supporting sub-contract and supplier documents that are available.
- Be careful in recommending contractors to clients.
- Ensure contract and tender documents match completely. Any variation in requirements will lead to disputes.
- Avoid, if at all possible, starting work on site before the contract documents are agreed and preferably signed. Be very careful with 'letters of intent'.
- Be clear as to your responsibilities under the contract and carry them out efficiently within the time limits imposed by the contract.
- Ensure your client is aware of their obligations under the contract they sign with the contractor.
- Neither you nor your client can afford to change your mind unless unavoidable.
- Keep accurate records of information supply and site progress and confirm all instructions in writing.
- Monitor costs constantly. Neither you nor your client wants nasty surprises when the building is completed.
- Site visits are to inspect work in progress as well as to attend meetings to discuss progress.
- Have all the information required for you to make a fair and reasonable decision on extension of time claims.

CONTINUED ▶

SUMMARY (CONTINUED)

- Ensure your certificates are fair and proper valuations of work in progress and do not include defective work.
- Take care when issuing the practical completion certificate, whatever the pressures from clients or contractors.
- You cannot issue a final certificate until you have agreed the final account. Ensure all known defects for which the contractor is liable have been rectified before issuing the final certificate.
- Keeps files for 15 years, just in case of problems or queries.

As your fees for administrating the building contract are almost certainly fixed, if the contract gets into serious trouble you will lose money on this part of your work. If it runs smoothly, you will make a profit, and everyone else involved will also be very happy!

Section 5
Keeping out of trouble with the law

There are more High Court cases in construction than in any other industry except shipping. Avoid being part of one of them!

Your risk exposure

Practising architecture is a very high-risk business. Apart from the normal business risks – getting sufficient work, uncertain clients, staffing problems and avoiding financial loss – you have a risk exposure to legal claims for negligence for alleged defects in buildings you design, not only from your clients but also from anyone who considers they have suffered damage or injury as a result.

Your clients can sue you for breach of contract if you do not provide them with the quality of architectural services you contracted to provide. But you are also exposed to claims under the law of tort from 'third parties': people with whom you have no contract but who allege they have suffered damage as a result of your actions or inaction.

The risk of you being sued for negligence is even greater. Architects are often the only people left (everyone else involved having gone bust or disappeared) for clients and others to sue when things go wrong. Also, there is the risk of being included in a 'blunderbuss' claim (writ), which includes anyone and everyone involved irrespective of who may be responsible for the problem.

Revised legal procedures have reduced this risk to a degree. The courts now require the parties to show evidence that they have attempted to settle their differences before setting in motion time-consuming and expensive legal actions.

Civil actions for damages are expensive and time consuming to defend, even if you are innocent.

In addition, you are exposed to increasing liability for criminal charges for breaches of statutory requirements, such as health and safety regulations, building regulations, town planning and listed building law. All can result in heavy fines or, in extreme circumstances, prison sentences.

The case of a public-sector architect charged with manslaughter as a result of a legionnaires' disease outbreak (she was found guilty initially, although that decision was reversed eventually on appeal) is a warning of the heavy responsibility architects can carry in terms of health and safety.

See also:
The ARB's
responsibilities,
page 129
Another risk area is the Architects Registration Board (ARB), which now has the responsibility for disciplining architects for not only 'unacceptable professional conduct' but also for 'serious professional incompetence'. The ARB has the power not only to suspend or erase your registration as an architect but also to impose fines.

Earlier sections of this guide have dealt with how to avoid problems in some of the key areas of your work. This section will help you to avoid falling foul of the law by helping you to understand your potential liabilities and identify how the risks to which you are exposed can be avoided, or at least minimised.

Your duty of care

As a 'professional', your legal responsibility is a 'reasonable duty of care' to your clients, with whom you have a contractual relationship. Other persons or organisations with whom you have no contract (you may not be aware of their existence) who claim they have suffered damages or injury because of your alleged negligent act may sue you 'in the tort' of negligence.

However, because your legal responsibility is no more than to take reasonable care, the fact that part of your building does not work properly is not proof in itself that you have been negligent. If you carried out the design and inspection of its erection with the degree of competence to be expected from an average architect, you will have a good defence against a claim of negligence.

Fitness for purpose

Contractors (and anyone supplying goods) carry a wider responsibility. The building they construct must be 'fit for its intended purpose'. If the roof leaks, irrespective of the reason, they are liable as the building is not fit for its intended purpose. If you buy a car and it does not work properly, it is defective and must be repaired or replaced. The car maker (or supplier) cannot avoid this responsibility by claiming they did their best but the problem could not reasonably have been anticipated and the defect was beyond their control.

This can be illustrated with the liability of dentists. When they extract or fill your teeth, dentists are providing a service with a 'reasonable duty of care' liability. When the same dentist makes you false teeth, these are classed as 'goods'. If they do not fit properly, they are 'not fit for the purpose' and must be replaced. Dentists cannot claim they did their best to make them fit.

It is important you do not drift into a situation where you take on the 'fitness for purpose' liability. Your professional indemnity insurance (PII) policy only covers you for professional negligence relating to your responsibility for 'reasonable duty of care'.

If you are employed by a contractor under a design–build contract, they may be carrying a fitness for purpose liability for their finished building. They may attempt to draw you into this increased liability through the design work you carry out for them. With the Contractor's Designed Portion of JCT 11 standard design–build forms the contractor's design liability is reduced to 'reasonable duty of care', although clients will not necessarily agree to this.

Also, if you are tempted to take a contractual responsibility for building the work you have designed, you will be operating as a design–build contractor. While this is permitted under the ARB's and the RIBA's codes of conduct (providing you are not at the same time acting as an independent advisor to the client), you must inform your PII provider in advance to ensure your PII policy covers you for this work.

The insurer may refuse to cover you if things go wrong and you have not obtained their agreement, or later when you notify them you have a 'fitness for purpose' claim, which is very difficult to defend. Your liability and normal PII cover is for 'reasonable duty of care', for which the defence is that you took reasonable care.

Civil law claims

These come under three main headings:

• Claims from those to whom you owe money for services or products.

- Claims from your clients for breach of contract, alleging your professional negligence in carrying out your role as architect and any associated duties that you agreed to perform.
- Claims from 'third parties' who you may not even be aware exist but who allege that something you have done (or not done) has caused them damage.

Claims for unpaid debts

If you run your practice efficiently, have a realistic business plan, monitor your finances carefully, keep your bank up to date with your financial position and do not take unwarranted risks, you should avoid serious problems with debtors.

If you are short of cash, first talk to your bank as they should help you (provided they are satisfied your position is not far worse than you are claiming). Always keep them informed in advance if you anticipate any financial pressure. It shows them you are in control of your business and should mean that they will help you with your cash-flow problems. Do not overlook the fact that in discussions with them your bank will, based on their records and your bank statements, have a fairly clear idea of your financial position and how you handle money.

Consider increasing your overdraft so that you can pay numerous pressing debtors and then have just one problem – how to pay off the overdraft! However, also examine your fee collection procedures. Is your cash-flow crisis being caused by not getting your accounts out on time or by you not chasing late payers? If so, read again the advice on getting paid in Section 2 of this guide.

Be as honest as you can with firms to whom you owe money. If you have a record for being a good payer, they will be helpful. If you have allowed significant debt to build up in the past, they will be less inclined to help. If your creditors are very difficult, negotiate a payment schedule that you can realistically maintain and keep to.

Avoid the pain of being taken to court for debts. It will be a stain on your credit worthiness, which may come back to haunt you later.

Breach of contract claims by your clients

If you are negligent in carrying out your duties to a client, you are in breach of contract. Your client can sue you for the damages they consider they have suffered as a result of your negligence. They have 6 years (12 years if the contract is a legal deed) from the date of the breach of contract in which to serve a claim (writ) on you, otherwise the claim will be deemed by the courts as out of time and unenforceable.

The date on which the six-year (or 12-year) limitation of claims 'clock' starts ticking is crucial. During construction there may be a number of separate problems, which give rise to negligence claims for design or construction defects at different times. As a general rule, assume you are not clear of a breach of contract claim until six (or 12) years after you have issued the practical completion certificate. With certain situations, such as rectification of defects, the limitation clock may not start until the final certificate is issued.

If you are designing residential projects, be aware of the provisions of the Defective Premises Act 1972, which has a 'fitness for purpose' liability as the premises have to be fit for habitation on completion, with a time limit on claims of six years from completion.

Avoid restarting the clock. If you return to your building after issuing your final certificate to advise on rectification of defects, you may restart the limitation period for another six or 12 years from the date of your last advice.

Most negligence claims will be made by your clients. Earlier sections of this guide have explained how, if you look after your clients, carefully control the design development of the project and competently carry out your duties under the building contract, you maximise the chances of avoiding negligence claims.

If you are unlucky and receive a claim, or are dragged into one through mistakes made by others, your best protection (although not total) is PII. This covers you for damages awarded against you (up to the limit of your cover) in the courts plus the legal fees involved. You have to pay the excess you carry on your policy.

Any amount awarded above your insurance cover is a charge against your personal assets, unless you restricted by agreement with your clients your liability for such claims or were operating as a limited liability company when appointed architect for the project.

Claims by third parties

As mentioned earlier in this section, third parties bring a considerable number of claims against architects. People or companies with whom you have no contract cannot sue for breach of contract. Their claims are 'in tort'.

You cannot restrict your liability against these claims in advance as you will not know the identity of the claimants until after the event giving rise to the claim. With a car accident you do not know the injured pedestrian or owner of the other damaged car until after the accident occurs. The courts award the victim whatever compensation they consider justified, which, as third party car insurance is compulsory, the insurance company pays.

You are open for claims 'in tort' for at least six years from the date the damage arises or when the client should reasonably have been aware of the defect. If a claim (writ) is not issued within six years, it is out of time and cannot be pursued.

The interpretation of this time limit by the courts has varied widely over the years. This uncertainty continues, and in theory liability can be virtually unlimited in time. The Latent Defects Act 1986 does, however (unless you have been guilty of deliberately covering up defects), limit the time in which a claim must be brought to 15 years from the date of the negligent act. This cut-off does not apply to personal injury resulting from negligence.

Personal injury claims

Time limits for personal injury claims are different. An injured person has three years to make a claim from the time they are aware of the injury or illness. However, as the effects of injury or illness may take many years to appear or develop into serious ill health, the courts have the power to extend the start date of the three years almost indefinitely. This is to ensure that an injury or illness the claimant could not reasonably have been aware of is not debarred by the 'out of time' limitation. This is how asbestos claims arising from previous decades are settled now.

Criminal charges

Architects' risks in the area of criminal law are increasing. Take great care to avoid getting into trouble with criminal law – the fines can be heavy, and in extreme cases you can go to prison!

You cannot insure against fines imposed as a result of criminal convictions or the financial consequences of being imprisoned. You can, however, insure to cover the legal defence costs if they are not already covered by your PII policy.

The ARB can suspend or erase your name from the Register of Architects if you are convicted of a criminal offence connected with, or reflecting on, your integrity as an architect, and can impose a fine or reprimand as a result of a criminal conviction that has material relevance to your fitness to practise as an architect. A conviction for dishonesty or fraud, even if not directly related to your practice, would result in ARB taking action. Motoring offences, unless very serious, are unlikely to warrant ARB action.

See also:
The Architects
code, *page*
130

Statutory breaches

Clients, as the property owners, are normally charged with breaches of town planning, building and similar regulations. Fines for breaches can be very heavy for each day the breach continues. If the breach was a result of your advice, action or inaction, you may be open to a claim for negligence from your clients.

To avoid these problems, ensure any actions by your clients of which you are aware (or should be aware) and which may involve breaches of statutory requirements are clearly against your advice, confirmed in writing. It is unlikely to be good enough for you to have looked the other way when the offence was being committed!

Town planning law

Breaches are most likely to be the illegal use of land or property or non-compliance with planning conditions. If you are aware of breaches, draw these to your client's attention and advise them in writing of the consequences to them of continuing.

If unauthorised work starts on site, the planning authority can issue a 'stop' notice on the property owner, requiring an immediate cessation of building work. If this is a result of you not having dealt with conditions attached to the planning consent requiring approval before work started, the client may have a claim for negligence against you for delays and extra costs.

Listed buildings

There is at least one case where an architect was charged with unauthorised work to a listed building. Check the status of any building that you have been commissioned to alter before work commences. Advise your clients of the approvals required and the penalties of non-compliance. It will normally be your responsibility to ensure that all necessary approvals are obtained and all conditions adhered to before work starts.

If the condition of the building when work starts makes it difficult, or even impossible, to comply with listed building consent, do not allow your client to use this as an excuse for demolishing or altering the building without obtaining specific consent to do so.

Similarly, do not allow parts of the listed building to be demolished because you consider them unsafe. If the building is in a dangerous condition, take temporary measures to remove the immediate danger, but do this with the agreement of the local authority building surveyor and in discussion with the local planning officer and English Heritage. Then agree a permanent solution.

Conservation areas

Special conditions apply for work to, or demolition of, buildings or development in conservation areas, which may include removal of permitted development rights. Approval is also required to fell trees in conservation areas. Do not allow your clients to proceed with demolition or any work that requires conservation area approval without a specific planning consent. If they do, make sure it is entirely at their risk and not yours.

Trees

Check for any 'protected' trees on your clients' sites. You are not allowed to do anything significant to them without specific approval.

Health and safety regulations

This is an area where architects' exposure to criminal charges is increasing. The Construction (Design and Management) Regulations contain a number of specific duties on the architect as the designer and specifier. There are other health and safety regulations which, although not necessarily your direct responsibility, you need to check carefully so you can identify breaches by others. You may get drawn in should the worst happen.

"Health and safety prosecutions are difficult to defend."

Remember, a breach of health and safety regulations may result in death, personal injury or long-term illness. The time limit for bringing these claims can be far longer than other negligence claims, and the damages awarded by the courts (as seen in car accident cases) can be very much higher.

Health and safety prosecutions are difficult to defend.

Access for disabled people

There are statutory requirements for buildings to be reasonably accessible to disabled people. 'Disabled' means far more than being in a wheelchair. It covers other impairments, such as blindness and deafness. The building regulations, which as the architect you are responsible for complying with, include disability access issues. Make sure you comply – later changes will be expensive to your client.

Other disabled access legislation (for example the Equality Act 2010 and the Disability Discrimination Act 1995) places the responsibility for ensuring buildings are accessible on the property owner. Most importantly, think 'accessibility' from the earliest of design stages. If you make it an 'add on' later, it may not work very well and will be more expensive and disruptive to the work on site

Reducing your liability risks

If you operate as a sole practitioner, you carry unlimited personal liability. If you are a partner, you are jointly and severally liable for claims with your partners. There is no such thing as an equal partnership. If disaster strikes and you have a claim not covered by PII, you all pay up jointly and then individually until the money runs out. The most affluent partner continues paying until his or her money runs out.

If you operate efficiently, with all the necessary check systems in place to identify errors and omissions before they become more than just a problem, your exposure to civil claims or criminal charges will be significantly reduced.

Risk assessment

However well you may be organised, you can only reduce your exposure to claims, not eliminate it. You may still find yourself with a serious negligence claim situation through no fault of your own.

So assess objectively and periodically where you are at risk in the various parts of your practice. Risks could arise through any of the following:

• falling workloads
• cash-flow problems
• high-profile projects
• difficult clients
• inefficient contractors

- staff shortages
- problems with internal communications
- technical errors by you or your partners/directors or staff.

Having identified the risks, decide how best you can remove them completely or, if this is not possible, at least reduce your exposure as much as you can. Question which risks are within your control and can be removed? Be aware of those over which you have no control so that you can avoid them.

The tripwires identified in this guide are all illustrations of the risk you carry of things going wrong. Avoid those tripwires and you will have removed or reduced your exposure to those risks.

Negligence claims

See also:
The proposal form, page 119 and Insurance premiums, page 120
The first way to reduce exposure to the financial consequences of the risks you carry is PII. However, that may not be sufficient to cover a catastrophic claim: if the risk was not notified at the right time, the claim may be 'voided' by your insurer, leaving you with no insurance cover for damages awarded or the legal costs as a result of that claim.

Also, it is possible (it *has* happened) that the insurance company issuing your policy may go bankrupt. In that case, if you are covered as a partnership or as an individual but not as a company, an insurance protection scheme may cover 90 per cent of any claim against you. To avoid losing cover completely it is wise to have a spread of cover with a number of companies or underwriters if possible. Your PII broker can advise you on this.

Other risks to be aware of are that the claim may be bigger than the level of your insurance cover, or by the time a claim is settled inflation will have taken the damages beyond the cover that was available in the year the claim was notified.

Limiting your liability by agreement with your client to, say, your agreed level of PII cover reduces the risk of a catastrophic claim from your client. However, you cannot limit your liability to claims from third parties.

As a sole practitioner or a partnership, claims not covered by your PII become claims against your personal assets, which can result in you being made personally bankrupt – a risk you must avoid, or at least minimise.

Consider very carefully operating as a limited liability company. The following are the salient points that should be borne in mind when considering changing to a limited liability company from sole practitioner or partnership to reduce your extreme risk exposure.

- By reducing your personal liability, a limited liability company almost certainly protects you from being made personally bankrupt in the event of a catastrophic claim, unless you can be specifically identified as the individual responsible for the negligence. You may lose your practice and the capital invested in it, but your personal assets cannot be used to pay the excess damages.
- Limited liability company status protects you from having to carry the personal liability for negligence by your partners (as in partnerships).
- If you convert, do remember that as a director you must be careful not to give personal guarantees and you must avoid situations where you take on a personal liability for any of your actions as a director, which can lead to a claim on you personally.
- You still need to have appropriate PII cover as a company, and it should cover retrospectively all previous work carried out by you or your previous partners.
- A company structure is a more flexible practice vehicle in which to operate than a partnership. Making a partner (and 'retiring' them if they are unsatisfactory) is a very complex and potentially painful operation.
- Operating as a company has tax advantages, although these can change. What may be an advantage or disadvantage today may not be so after next year's budget!
- You must take specialist legal and tax advice before deciding to move from sole practitioner or partnership to a limited company structure.

Bear in mind that as a company you have to file annual accounts at Companies House, so the world will know how well or badly you are faring financially.

The protection of the limited company status only operates from when the company starts operating. You have not limited your liability for any claims that may arise from work you carried out before you set up the company. So the advice to those starting in practice is to start as a limited company.

You may be able to cover the work you carried out prior to operating with limited liability under your company PII policy, but you will still be exposed personally to claims for damages above the level of your cover.

Finally, when you switch to a limited company you must notify all your existing clients and obtain their agreement to changing their contract from you personally to the new company. That is normally not a problem as most of your clients deal with limited liability companies constantly and unless you have on-going problems with them they are unlikely to object.

Limited liability partnerships

Normal partnerships are of individuals responsible severally and jointly for the partnership's actions. Companies are separate legal entities, where the shareholders are not responsible personally for the company's debts. The Limited Liability Partnerships Act 2000 created a new halfway house, between the traditional partnership, with personal unlimited liability, and the limited liability company. It was created primarily to meet the needs of accountants and auditors, who were facing potentially enormous personal liability claims for negligent auditing of large failed companies. It limits each partner's personal liability but retains the essence of a partnership rather than a commercial company.

Partnerships that do not wish to convert to a limited company should consider converting to a limited liability partnership as a means of restricting their exposure to a catastrophic claim. The process of conversion is similar to converting to a company. However, as with changing to limited company status, it is essential to take expert legal and taxation advice before coming to any decision to convert. Taxation is as for partnerships so there are unlikely to be any tax advantages in converting.

SUMMARY

- You are in a very high-risk business. In addition to the normal business risks, you are exposed to legal claims for negligence in breach of contract from your clients, and third party claims 'in tort' by anyone else who can claim you have caused them damage or injury.
- Your exposure to criminal charges, which can result in heavy fines and, in extreme cases, prison, is increasing.
- Your professional responsibility is a 'reasonable duty of care' – to do your best. Be careful not to drift into situations where your liability has increased to 'fitness for purpose' – you will then have increased your potential liability exposure, which may not be covered by your PII.

CONTINUED ▶

SUMMARY (CONTINUED)

- The time limit for claims for negligence varies, but it can continue for up to 15 years after practical completion of your building. In the case of personal injury claims, it is normally three years, but can be very much longer if the consequences of the injury do not emerge until much later.
- Be very careful not to be involved in breaches of statutory requirements. Criminal charges with heavy fines and, in extreme cases, prison sentences can be the punishment.
- Be aware of the risks to which you are exposed. Operate your practice with maximum efficiency and have check systems in place to pick up mistakes before they become major problems.
- Take out and maintain the maximum PII cover you can reasonably afford. Make sure it is not 'voided', leaving you without cover against a claim. Increase the cover as your workload grows and ensure it is in line with inflation.
- Limit your liability with your client where possible to an agreed level of PII cover.
- Consider seriously the benefits of practising through a limited liability company or limited liability partnership to virtually remove the risk of a catastrophic claim making you personally bankrupt.

Understand your legal responsibilities and keep up to date with changes in the law, both through new legislation and High Court decisions. High Court decisions may change the interpretation of current law and increase your risk exposure!

Section 6

Keeping out of trouble with professional indemnity insurance

You need to sleep at night! So, you must insure against negligence claims from your clients and from anyone else who may consider themselves damaged by your error or omission.

The architect's exposure to damages claims

Practising architecture is a high-risk business. Virtually every building designed, despite the increased use of standardised components, is a 'one-off'. A large number of people of widely different skills and experience are involved in design and construction. If the roof leaks, your client may claim damages from you. If a piece of the outside cladding of the building you have designed falls and injures a passer-by, you may, as with a car accident, have a very large third party personal injury claim from someone you do not know and have never met.

The number of things that can go wrong is immeasurable. A very big claim could bankrupt you.

There are various ways to reduce your exposure to these potential disasters. Covering as much as possible of your risk exposure by insurance, as with your house and car driving, is an obvious safeguard. Limiting your liability by agreement with your client or by practising as a limited liability company or a limited liability partnership are further possibilities.

Professional indemnity insurance (PII)

You must have PII cover because:

- Architecture is a high-risk occupation. You can be sued (or brought into claims against others involved in the project) not only by your clients but also by a wide range of third parties. You are every solicitor's first potential target (and sometimes the only one left!) when deciding who to claim against when something has gone wrong.
- Most 'sophisticated' clients will require you to have insurance cover to a minimum amount that they specify before they will commission you as the architect. They may also require confirmation that you are covered to that level. Check with your PII provider before giving clients any details.
- However well organised and efficient your architectural practice is, you will not be immune to the claims that may not even be your fault and which you will need to defend. *Proving your innocence can be expensive if you do not have insurance cover.*
- PII cover should be a positive selling point in negotiating fees for small projects with 'lay' clients, who might be tempted to accept an undercut fee from a 'cowboy' with no PII cover. With these smaller one-off clients, you should emphasise, diplomatically, that should things go badly wrong, you have insurance for their protection.
- The ARB's code of conduct Standard 8 requires you to have insurance cover to adequate and appropriate levels if you are practising using the title 'architect'. Until 2010 the ARB required you to confirm that you had specified minimum levels of PII cover, and over previous years there is a long list of architects being struck off for not providing evidence they had PII cover. While this was not an onerous requirement, pressure to remove this requirement lead to it being withdrawn in 2010. However, both the ARB and the RIBA (if you are an RIBA Registered Practice) still require you to have adequate and appropriate PII. If a complaint is made against you to the ARB and it is then discovered you do not have adequate required cover, that will be a factor taken into account in dealing with the complaint.

  See:
  ARB
  disciplinary
  procedures,
  page 133

- If you were to negotiate with your client to proceed with the project without PII cover, this still leaves you exposed to third party claims (which if they involve personal injury can be very high), which must be covered in the public interest.
- The ARB also advises that employed architects should as far as possible ensure that PII cover or other appropriate cover is provided by their employer. It is in your interests if you are a public or private employee to check with your employer that PII cover is in place and that you as an employee are covered. It is possible in extreme circumstances for you to be sued for a negligent act you committed while employed in that office, even after you have left!

- If you are employed and take on 'one-off' projects, you still need in your own interests to be covered by PII. This may be best resolved by persuading your employer to include your occasional work on their PII policy. This is unlikely to increase their annual premium and should normally be accepted by their insurer without difficulty. Do obtain written confirmation that you are covered by their policy in case you have a potential claim that must be notified. Otherwise you will need a PII policy for any 'one-off' or part-time work, such as the RIBASur policy provided by the RIBA Insurance Agency.

Be aware that the ARB issues a helpful guide to PII (*Guidelines and Information: Professional Indemnity Insurance*). While the ARB does not now prescribe minimum levels of PII it does emphasise the need for all practising architects to carry adequate and appropriate PII cover and Standard 8 of its code of conduct makes it clear that you are expected to have adequate and appropriate PII cover, including 'run-off' cover, in place to cover your practice and employees. You are advised to notify your client you hold PII cover at the outset of the project when you agree your terms of reference.

"Both ARB and RIBA codes require you to have PII cover without specifying specific levels if a complaint is made against you and it emerges you do not have appropriate cover this will be a factor in deciding the complaint against you. "

The RIBA requires all RIBA Registered Practices (as opposed to individual architects) to have appropriate PII cover. The RIBA *Code of Professional Conduct* Guidance Note 5, which deals with insurance, states at clause 5.1:

> *Members practising architecture are exposed to the risk of being sued for negligence or breaches of contract. Some form of insurance should therefore be held which will generally cover liabilities arising from such claims.*

Clause 5.5 goes on:

> *Members should therefore ensure that their professional work is protected by an appropriate insurance policy at a level of cover commensurate with the type of projects they undertake.*

Annex GN5 attached to the guidance note does not claim to cover all the intricacies of PII, merely the main points, but it is a useful general explanation of PII. Holding appropriate insurance cover is a requirement if you wish to be an RIBA Registered Practice.

What cover do you require?

You cannot afford not to have the maximum cover you can reasonably afford that covers each and every potential claim that might be made against you. In any event, some clients will specify the PII level you must have if they are to commission you on their project.

If you are a sole practitioner or practise part-time on your own you may feel you cannot afford the cost of PII however, you cannot afford not to be covered, any more than you can afford not to insure your house or drive a car without adequate cover against the unintended or unexpected.

The RIBA Insurance Agency provides a range of low-cost and ARB-compliant insurance policies for RIBA members who do part-time or small-scale work. *If you do not have PII and are in practice then think hard about what you will do when a potential claim arrives.*

PII policies are for one year at a time and are on a 'claims made' basis. They only cover you for claims made during that year. If your practice is growing, that should not represent a problem and you should increase your cover as your workload and risk exposure increases. Take cover for 'each and every claim' otherwise you could be unlucky and have more than one very large claim in a single year and find the second claim is not fully covered.

Cover all your professional work. Make sure the policy covers all types of 'architectural' work you carry out and covers all your previous practices, partners and work. If you operate as a planning supervisor or disabled access consultant or undertake any other related architectural activity, make sure you inform your insurer and that they confirm you are covered for the 'additional services' you are providing.

Reducing cover

If you are in a downturn situation it is very unwise to reduce the level of your PII cover as claims that may subsequently arise will be on work you carried out in previous years, when you were very busy and profitable. Reducing cover should be the last resort as you are risking not being fully covered if a big claim arises from work you carried out in previous years.

Excesses

Take the highest reasonable 'excess' (you pay this first amount of every settled claim, similar to car insurance), but remember that if you have more than one claim, you pay that amount against each proved claim made against you. As a notified potential claim to your insurer creates a potential liability to pay the excess amount in your policy, discuss with your accountant whether this can be dealt with in your annual accounts as a contingent liability and can therefore be a legitimate charge against profits.

Who should be covered?

Obviously, if you are a sole practitioner, you individually must be covered, along with any staff you employ. Even for any part-time work you may do outside your main employment, or if 'semi-retired', you must be covered.

With partnerships, you should identify all present partners individually as well as the collective name of the partnership. Include all previous partnerships and partners.

If you are a limited liability company, you need to cover the company, the directors and previous directors or partnerships before incorporation. It is advisable to cover the directors individually, for if your PII company should go bust (it has happened) the Insurance Industry Protection Scheme will normally cover individuals, but not a company, for up to 90 per cent of claims. This is particularly important if you are a sole practitioner operating as a limited company.

So cover everyone and everything who is and was involved!

Retired partners

Retired partners will continue to be potentially liable (for a minimum of six years and up to 15 years) for alleged negligence that arose while they were in practice. All 'retired' partners should therefore also be covered by your PII policy. You will be able to set the cost against tax, whereas they, as retired people with no earned practice income, cannot.

If you are a retired partner, ensure your continuing practice PII policy covers you against all claims while the practice continues. Ensure your retirement agreement excludes you from responsibility to provide a share of any policy excesses that have to be paid as a result of a successful claim. If your original practice goes out of business before you have been retired for 15 years, you should take out your own 'run-off' policy for the remaining period. As the risks will be low, the premium should not be very great.

Be clear that 'retired' in this since means retired from that practice and not necessarily retirement due to advancing age!

Retired sole practitioners

If you retire as a sole practitioner (either through advancing age or to take up salaried employment) you will need to take out 'run-off' insurance to cover you against any claims that may arise after you have ceased private practice. Relatively inexpensive policies are available. Discuss with your accountant whether you can organise this so that it is tax deductible.

Retired directors

In reality it is unlikely that a claim for negligence while you were acting as a director of your company would be successful, unless you can be specifically identified as the individual responsible for the negligent act. However, the law is beginning to extend the potential liability of individual employees for negligent acts, so similar requirements to those for retired partners apply. Ensure your previous company's PII policy continues to cover you personally, and if for any reason it does not, take out 'run-off' cover.

Policy extensions

The costs of fee recovery are a standard extension to cover, however it can be a double-edged benefit. Some clients react to claims for fees by immediately alleging negligence – your insurer will have the responsibility of dealing with both claims. Experience indicates that unless the fee claim is for a very high figure (and the legal expenses for recovery very high) settlement is probably best negotiated between you and your client and not left to indemnity insurers unless it is part of a very much larger negligence claim.

Other extensions that are either offered as standard by many policies or involve an additional premium cover include:

- defamation
- loss of documents
- copyright infringement.

If there is no extra cost, take them; otherwise, question whether are they worth the extra premium.

Policy exclusions

You are only covered in the work areas specified in your policy. If you are carrying out work overseas or in 'single-project partnerships' this must be specifically disclosed and cover may be refused or attract an extra premium. If not disclosed and accepted by your insurer, it will almost certainly not be covered retrospectively should a claim against you arise.

Your insurer may not be prepared to cover you for overseas work, particularly in the litigation-mad USA! You must inform your insurer of any overseas work before you start to ensure you are covered by your existing PII policy. There may be an extra premium to pay to cover the risk.

Criminal charges

Architects' exposure to criminal charges in relation to their architectural practice is increasing. Listed buildings, building regulations and particularly health and safety regulations are examples where serious breaches of statutory provisions can lead to criminal charges. You cannot insure against fines or other losses arising from criminal convictions. However, consider obtaining seperate insurance cover for legal defence costs for criminal charges.

The proposal form

PII is based on annual policies. Each year the policy is a new policy, possibly with a new mix of underwriters. It is a policy based on 'absolute good faith' – this is the obligation on you to disclose to your insurer all facts that are known to you and not known to them that may influence the level of the insurance cover they provide and the premium they charge.

That obligation starts from when you complete the proposal form. Any matter that arises in the period between proposal and acceptance that may affect the cover being offered must be notified to the insurer. Not to do so may lead to your insurer refusing to cover particular claims if they consider there has not been full disclosure.

Even worse, they can 'void' a whole annual policy, refuse to cover any claims during that year and return the premium you paid for cover that they have withdrawn. If that happens, you do not have insurance cover for what is by then a known claim, which will have to be defended and, if proved, will have to be paid out of your own pocket.

The proposal form must be completed with great care to ensure nothing that is likely to be relevant is overlooked. This is the information you provide to enable the insurer to decide the appropriate premium to cover your risks for the coming year. However, while you must be entirely truthful, you are entitled to complete the proposal form to show your practice in the best, and not the worst, light.

Use an insurance broker who specialises in this type of insurance. Use their expertise to help you fill in the form. Size of contracts completed, types of building (some are a higher risk than others) and fee income for various types of work are vital information, which must be as accurate as possible.

"Your policy proposal form is the basis of your cover. Make sure you get it right!"

You must disclose in the proposal form all 'circumstances that have led or are likely to lead to a claim'. If they have been notified to the insurer in previous years they should be covered by those policies and are merely included to establish your claims record.

If potential claims have not been notified at the proper time, and certainly before renewal, the insurer may refuse cover on the basis that they should have been notified under an earlier policy. Specifically, they are unlikely to cover a claim or potential claim that was not disclosed to them on the proposal form as this will have denied them the opportunity to either refuse cover or charge a higher premium.

Your policy proposal form is the basis of your cover. Make sure you get it right!

Insurance premiums

The market for PII fluctuates. New insurers may enter the market and offer lower premiums. At other times, insurers may withdraw, the market hardens and premiums rise.

Cover is usually in layers, with one underwriter taking the first slice of the total risk insured and others taking various percentages of the remainder. This 'mix' of insurers can mean that although you think you have renewed your cover with the same insurer, that may not be absolutely correct. It is preferable to have your cover in layers, for should the insurance company covering the whole of your risk go bankrupt, the whole of your cover could disappear overnight.

It is wise to get at least two quotes, but do not contemplate changing your insurer unless there is a big saving. Check the policy wording: a cheaper quote may not give the same cover and may be stricter in application. However, it is possible to negotiate cover, and most insurers agree to staged premium payments to help your cash flow.

If you intend to change, be absolutely certain all circumstances that might lead to a claim have been notified to your present insurer before the policy expires. Otherwise, you may create a situation where there is a dispute between your previous and new insurers as to who should be responsible for a claim.

Continuity in cover with one insurer is important as it helps to protect you – although not completely – from disputes as to which year's policy a claim may fall into.

Policy wording

When you receive quotations for the level of cover you require, check the policy wording carefully to ensure it covers all the risks and everyone you specified in the proposal form. Ensure you are covered for all the work you carry out, or intend to carry out, that may be in addition to the normal work of an architect. Acting as a planning supervisor, adjudicator, client design adviser or expert witness are obvious additional risks, which insurers might not cover unless they have agreed to do so in advance.

Check for clauses that require you to include disclaimers in any condition or structural surveys relating to, for example, wood rot. Ensure everyone in the practice is aware of all special requirements and check periodically that they are complied with; otherwise, you may not be covered by your insurance.

As with all insurance policies, the small print can be very important – so read it. If you are not clear as to its meaning, ask your broker to explain.

Notifications of potential claims to your insurer

Your obligation is to immediately notify your insurer of all circumstances that may give rise to a claim against you. This includes, in most policies, a requirement, for example, for you to notify them within 48 hours of any adjudication notice you receive. Insurers are very concerned about decisions of adjudicators and need to be informed of what is happening, taking into account the very short time-scale for an adjudicator to give a decision on a dispute and the legal implications of that decision.

In a busy practice, circumstances that might give rise to a claim can easily be overlooked, so institute procedures (or discipline yourself if you are a sole practitioner) to ensure you are aware of and can monitor all problems before they reach the stage where you need to notify your insurer.

Monthly partners' or directors' meetings offer an ideal opportunity to check for problems. You should have a specific agenda item for every meeting to check with everyone that there are no problems on any projects or contracts that could conceivably lead to a claim. Decide then whether the matter warrants an immediate notification to the insurer through your broker. If you do not do so, monitor the situation carefully, keep your broker informed and get them to notify the insurer as soon as it is clear you have a potential claim situation.

Keeping a potential claims 'smoke list' can also be helpful. In your meeting agenda, keep a list (which comes up automatically each meeting) of problems that should be recorded in case they develop into serious issues that may need notification. As and when they are resolved and no longer a problem, take them off the list.

Above all, at meetings that fall immediately before the renewal of your PII policy is due, make absolutely sure everyone owns up to any problem areas. Confirm individually with partners and staff that there are no problems that have arisen which could lead to a negligence claim which should be considered for notification.

If there are any problems that you feel may warrant notification, discuss them with the specialist insurance broker who has placed the PII for you. They are experts and have a duty to advise you on the best course of action – use them. They also have PII for negligence!

If you leave notification until the problem becomes a claim you may find that the insurer refuses cover because the problem should have been notified in a previous year to another insurer. The previous insurer may then refuse cover, as they were not notified during the life of their policy. You will then be personally liable not only to meet the claim but also the costs of your defence. Even if you win, you will almost certainly bear some of the costs.

If you are a sole practitioner, you must discipline yourself to note automatically any problems that have arisen and discuss possible notification with your PII broker. When coming up for policy renewal, ask yourself whether there are any notifications you should make before your present policy expires and it is too late. If you fail to notify a potential claim before your present annual policy expires, you may not be covered for later claims by your new policy.

Be careful with the wording of your notification, particularly if you have a number of problems on the same project that may eventually need to be notified. You have to avoid putting the insurer in a position where they treat each notification as a separate claim as you will then have a series of excess charges, rather than one claim and one excess payment when the claim is settled.

Do not be nervous about whether notifications will increase the premium when your PII policy is up for renewal. Unless they are numerous and significant, notifications are unlikely to increase your policy premium. Settled claims against you certainly do! Insurers take comfort if a practice is efficient in dealing with problems. They are nervous about architects who never notify. They know you cannot be that efficient – or that lucky.

The ARB *Guidance and Information* leaflet on PII has a good summary of when to notify.

The moment you have identified a potential claim situation discuss this with your PII broker and if in doubt – notify!

Dealing with claims

Your problems will be made worse if negligence claims are not handled with great care. Your first consideration must be to ensure you do nothing to put your insurance cover at risk. The time you spend on assisting insurers with the defence of a claim is lost time, but you must give this work priority to help defeat the claim or achieve a settlement.

Do not admit liability

When receiving a notice of a claim for negligence from a client (or any other source), as with car accidents, you must not admit liability. Be very careful not to prejudice your position and that of your insurer in any discussions with your client in an attempt to achieve a quick settlement. Make sure it is understood by everyone involved that all such discussions and correspondence are 'without prejudice'.

Notify immediately

You must notify your insurer without delay, and send them copies of all relevant correspondence. Do not wait for the claim (writ) to arrive!

Insurers handle claims, you do not! Once you have notified the insurer, the responsibility for dealing with the claim is no longer with you. The insurer will instruct solicitors. Your insurer should meet the cost of your defence, even if that takes the cost of the settlement or judgement above the limit of your cover.

While normally there should not be a conflict of interest for the solicitors acting for you and the insurer, it is the insurer, not you, who appoints the solicitors handling your claim. If you consider there to be a potential conflict of interest (the claim may, for example, be much higher than your cover limit or the insurer may be considering refusing cover) you can appoint your own solicitor, but you will have to bear their costs.

While the insurer will discuss issues with you through the solicitors as they arise, they have complete control of the case and can decide to settle (or not to settle) if they consider it appropriate to do so. Whether you think you are blameless and should not settle, or wish to settle to dispose of the case, it is usually wise to go along with the insurer's decision. If you want to proceed and not settle, you are on your own from then on. Whatever your outraged feelings of right and wrong, can you risk that?

Be totally honest with your solicitor. Be objective about your position. Do not believe what you want to believe. Misleading or withholding information from your solicitor makes things worse!

Non-disclosure

Do not disclose that you have PII cover without your insurer's permission unless you informed the client of its existence and level as a condition of being appointed to the commission.

Records

Check that your correspondence and job files are in order and complete as you will need to refer to them and make copies for the insurer's solicitors. Keep an accurate record of all meetings and discussions when they take place, whoever they may be with, in relation to the claim.

Even if you think it is a claim that is far less than your policy excess, do not attempt to negotiate a settlement without your insurer's agreement. If you do, you may prejudice your cover. What begins as a small claim can escalate into something much larger!

Disclosure of documents

Remember at all times that at some stage in the proceedings your solicitor will be obliged to disclose all your relevant documents to the other side. Documents between you and your solicitor will be privileged and do not have to be disclosed.

Always bear this in mind when writing letters, making diary entries, sending faxes and e-mails, taking minutes or holding telephone conversations, which in a legal case must be disclosed to the other side. Incautious internal memos, e-mails and letters to third parties can damage your case when disclosed to the other side. They will be looking for the 'whoopee' letter or document that proves their case.

Sensitive correspondence or meeting minutes with others in relation to the claim should, where possible, be conducted through your solicitor to avoid these documents having to be disclosed to the other side.

SUMMARY

- You cannot afford not to have PII. You are in a high-risk business, so take the highest reasonable cover you can afford. Ensure all your professional activities and all past and present partnerships, companies and individuals are covered.
- Follow the ARB guide on PII and ensure you comply with Standard 8 of the ARB code. If a RIBA Registered Practice, ensure you comply with the RIBA's requirements.

CONTINUED ▶

- Your PII policy is based on complete disclosure of all relevant facts, so ensure you do this when completing the proposal form. Use an insurance broker who specialises in the PII market and make use of their expertise.
- Do not change insurer without good reason. Continuity of cover should avoid any risk of a dispute between insurers as to which policy should cover a claim. Check policy wording carefully to ensure you have the cover requested in your proposal form.
- You must notify your insurer on any matter likely to give rise to a claim. Institute procedures in your practice to ensure potential claim issues are discussed regularly, and especially when policy renewal is imminent.
- Notifications do not increase the insurance premium, settled claims do. So, if in doubt – notify!
- The more comprehensive and detailed your records are, the better equipped you are to defeat a claim, or at least reduce your contribution to the negligence. But be careful with the wording of internal notes and e-mails.

However careful and efficient you are, you need PII to protect you from the unexpected. Without PII it can be very expensive to prove your innocence!

Section 7

Keeping out of trouble with the ARB and the RIBA

Both the ARB and the RIBA have codes of conduct for architects, and if you beach the codes they can discipline you: it is in your interests to understand the responsibilities of these bodies, the levels of conduct and performance that they expect of you and the sanctions that they can impose on you.

The title 'architect' is protected by law in the United Kingdom. Only those persons who are qualified and on the Register of Architects can practice using it. The Architects Registration Board (ARB) has powers not only to set standards for admission to the register but also to discipline architects for unacceptable professional conduct or serious professional incompetence. The ARB's protection of the title prevents builders, surveyors and every other Tom, Dick and Harry from using the title 'architect' – something that you spent seven long years of hard work and studying to obtain. So, if you want to practise within the UK using the title 'architect', keep out of trouble with the ARB.

The Royal Institute of British Architects (RIBA) has powers to discipline its members over matters of professional conduct. So, if you want to use the title 'chartered architect', be an RIBA Registered Practice, use the RIBA affix and make use of the many benefits of RIBA membership, keep out of trouble with the RIBA.

Of course, it is best to avoid problems in your professional activities by setting yourself high standards of professionalism and integrity and by ensuring that at all times the service you provide reaches the level of competence expected of an architect practising in the UK. Both the ARB and the RIBA have codes of conduct. Use them as good practice guides – because that is what they are.

The origins of registration

Registration goes back to the 1920s, a time when the profession was deeply divided on the issue. The 1931 and 1938 Architects Registration Acts were passed after heated debates in parliament and elsewhere. The Architects Registration Council UK (ARCUK) was set up after the 1931 Act with limited disciplinary powers, but it did not prevent the practice of architecture by unregistered persons, provided they did not do so using the title 'architect'.

The Architects Registration Board

Protecting the consumer and safeguarding the reputation of architects

Pressure for change in the early 1990s resulted in a government proposal to abolish protection of the title 'architect'. Following representation from consumer bodies, it was eventually decided that a new body, the Architects Registration Board (ARB), should replace the ARCUK. The ARB would have significantly increased powers to discipline incompetent architects and those acting unprofessionally.

Whereas the ARCUK had a 72-member representative and unelected governing council and a nearly as large separate Board of Architectural Education, the ARB has a much smaller governing council, comprising seven architects elected every three years from all architects on the ARB register and eight 'lay' members appointed by the Privy Council.

The Architects Act 1997 defines the role and responsibilities of ARB, not only in protecting the consumer but also in setting standards of competence and safe-guarding the reputation of the architectural profession. The new ARB came into being on 1 April 1997, primarily as a consumer protection body with far greater disciplinary powers than ARCUK.

The price the profession paid to maintain the protection of the title 'architect' was the creation of a consumer protection body with a lay member majority to ensure that architects are not only persons with professional integrity but are also competent in the service they provide to their clients.

Without the protection of title, anyone – tinker, tailor, builder, undertaker – would be able to call themselves 'architects'.

The ARB's responsibilities

The ARB only has jurisdiction over architects practising in the UK, although it has certain responsibilities in relation to European Union legislation where it affects architects, including representation on the Architects Council for Europe. As the UK statutory authority, the ARB has the following responsibilities.

1. **To maintain the register of people properly qualified to use the title 'architect'.**
    If you are off the register for more than two years you have to satisfy the ARB that you are still competent before you can be readmitted. Previously, under ARCUK architects who might not have practised for many years had an automatic right to be reinstated to the register at any time as 'qualified', even though they might be totally out of touch with current architectural practice. *So, do not lose your registration by being struck off the register by the ARB or by not paying your annual retention fee. You now have no automatic right to be readmitted to the register if you have been off it for more than two years.*

2. **To set the educational and professional practice standards to qualify for admission to the register.**
    The ARB has a statutory duty to oversee the education and training of architects to ensure they have reached an acceptable level of professional competence before they can be admitted to the register. This is carried out in co-operation with the RIBA and the architectural schools.

3. **To prosecute people using the title 'architect' who are not on the register.**
    It is not in your interests to see the unqualified usurping a title you have sweated seven years to acquire, so report any case that comes to your attention.

4. **To discipline architects who are found guilty of unacceptable professional conduct, serious professional incompetence or have a criminal conviction.**
    If the ARCUK was largely a toothless tiger, the ARB certainly is not. The ARB has a statutory duty to deal with complaints against architects under these headings. The ARB Professional Conduct Committee (PCC) has powers to reprimand or suspend you, erase your name from the register or fine you (up to £2,500) if you are found guilty of any of these offences.

Unacceptable professional conduct and serious professional incompetence

If your client considers that your actions constitute 'conduct which falls short of the standard required of a registered person' and makes a complaint to the ARB, unless the Registrar considers it to be trivial the complaint must be investigated. If there is a case to answer, you will have to defend yourself against a charge of 'unacceptable professional conduct' and/or 'serious professional incompetence'.

If the ARB notifies you of a complaint against you, however trivial or incorrect you may consider it, treat it seriously from the outset. Reply promptly to all notifications and correspondence from the ARB and do all you can to resolve the complaint.

Criminal convictions

You may also be disciplined by the ARB if you are convicted of a criminal offence, but only if that offence is relevant to your fitness to practise as an architect, which is determined as follows:

1.   It arises directly out of your professional activities.
2.   It results in a sentence of imprisonment, suspended or not.
3.   It constitutes an offence of dishonesty.
4.   It otherwise calls into question your integrity.

The Architects Code: Standards of Conduct and Practice (2010 version)

The ARB's professional code is published as *The Architects Code: Standards of Conduct and Practice (2010 version)*. ARB makes it clear that your failure to comply with the code does not necessarily lead to disciplinary proceedings, but that failure to follow its guidance would certainly be taken into account should it be necessary to examine your conduct or competence.

You are expected to follow the spirit of the code as well as its express terms. Therefore it follows that if a course of conduct complained about is not specifically referred to in the code, it can still be the subject of ARB disciplinary proceedings. Equally, a complaint alleging breach of the code will not necessarily result in disciplinary proceedings. Discipline cases are judged on the specific issues involved.

Read the ARB code not just as a code to be followed to keep you out of trouble with the ARB but also as a guide to good practice. The code does not repeat the obligations of general law, such as discrimination and employment law. The standards it requires you to achieve are no more than good practice management principles.

While the ARB's standards reflect the consumer protection role of the ARB, they are also a sound basis on which you should operate your practice.

The code comprises twelve standards setting general principles. The standards are amplified by explanatory notes.

- **Standard 1: Honesty and Integrity.** Architects should at all times act with integrity and avoid any action or situations which are inconsistent with their professional obligations.
  Respect confidentiality at all times, avoid conflicts of interest and do not practise with a disqualified person.

- **Standard 2: Competence.** Architects should only undertake professional work for which they are able to provide adequate professional, financial and technical competence and resources.
  Do not take on work you cannot carry out properly. Keep up to date.

- **Standard 3: Honesty.** Architects should only promote their professional services in a truthful and responsible manner.
  Promote your practice truthfully, do not mislead.

- **Standard 4: Competent Management.** Architects should carry out their professional work faithfully, conscientiously and with due regard to relevant technical and professional standards. Ensure at all times you have written terms of engagement and fee agreements with your clients and that these are updated by agreement when they change during the project.
  Use skill, care and diligence. Keep up to date. Keep to time and budgets set by your clients.

- **Standard 5: Consider Others.** In carrying out or agreeing to carry out professional work, architects should pay due regard to the interests of anyone who may reasonably be expected to enjoy or use the products of their own work.
  Remember that while your prime responsibility is to your clients, you do have wider responsibilities to society.

- **Standard 6: Competence.** Architects should maintain their professional service and competence in areas relevant to their professional work, and discharge the requirements of any engagement with commensurate knowledge and attention. *Keep up to date at all times with legislative, professional and technical changes. Continuing professional development (CPD) is important.*

- **Standard 7: Trustworthiness.** Architects should preserve the security of money entrusted to their care in the course of their practice or business.
  Do not treat your clients' money as though it were your own!

- **Standard 8: Insurance Arrangements.** Architects should not undertake professional work without adequate and appropriate insurance cover.
  You must have sufficient insurance cover for potential claims against you for negligence. It is as much in your interest as your clients'! The ARB until 2010 set compulsory minimum levels of PII cover, but these have been withdrawn. However, the ARB still requires you to have adequate cover and can ask you for evidence of this if a complaint is made against you. If retiring from practice you need to ensure your previous practice continues to cover you against any claims that may arise after you retire or that you take 'run-off' cover for a minimum of six years. See the ARB's Guidance and Information: Professional Indemnity Insurance.

- **Standard 9: Reputation of Architects.** Architects should ensure that their personal and professional finances are managed responsibly.
  Make sure you can financially carry the work you take on and, above all, avoid bankruptcy and paying judgment debts! If you get into financial trouble or are subject to a criminal conviction you have a duty to inform the ARB. This is also something of a whistle-blowers' charter as you are expected to inform the ARB of any architect who significantly falls below the ARB standards.
  If you are subject to an investigation by the ARB you must do all you can to assist that investigation.

- **Standard 10: Disputes and Complaints.** You are expected to have a written procedure for dealing with complaints and to notify this to clients. The ARB encourages you to use, wherever you can, alternative dispute resolution, such as mediation.
  If you allow disputes to fester, small issues can become bigger problems, and then disasters. You could then be in big trouble with your clients and the ARB.

- **Standard 11: Co-operation over Regulatory Requirements.** You are expected to co-operate with the ARB and provide all information required of you. Also do ensure any change of address is notified to the ARB as this can be a reason for being removed from the register.

- **Standard 12: Respect for Others.** Treat everyone you deal with fairly and in accordance with the law. Avoid discrimination of any kind.

If you decide to operate as a limited liability company or a limited liability partnership (LLP) and wish to include the word 'architect' or 'architects' in the name of the company or LLP you have to get approval from the ARB, which will be granted provided the ARB is satisfied that there is at least one registered architect who will be responsible for any architectural work carried out.

Dealing with clients' complaints to the ARB

Almost all complaints to the ARB flow from disagreements with clients. They usually have small beginnings, which are well flagged up in advance. It follows that the best way to avoid complaints to the ARB, which will cost you time and money, even if you are innocent, is to do all you can to resolve problems when they first arise.

- The ARB code sets out a procedure for dealing with complaints. Use it to defuse a situation that may otherwise become a major dispute and which could finish up in court and as a complaint about you to the ARB.
- If the complaint in any way suggests negligence on your part, even if you feel it is totally unjustified or of little consequence, notify your PII provider immediately through your specialist PII broker.
- Consider using the RIBA Conciliation Service to resolve complaints rapidly and amicably before attitudes on both sides become entrenched.

As clients cannot obtain damages from you without first going to court, a complaint to the ARB will most likely seek to have you punished for what the client considers to be your professional failures, to draw public attention to their complaint and perhaps to use a disciplinary decision against you as a basis of a negligence claim.

Beware of the client who feels wronged – rightly or wrongly – and seeks revenge! They become 'clients from hell'.

ARB disciplinary procedures

At the time of going to press the ARB Board were making important changes to the procedures for investigating complaints. The Investigation Committee comprising ARB Board members is being abolished and replaced by a pool of appointed "investigators" who are not ARB Board members who will investigate the complaint and decide whether the complaint should be referred to the Professional Conduct

Committee (PCC) for a hearing. This decision will be subject to the ARB Board's solicitor's power to request the Investigators to reconsider their decision if they do not consider that the architect has a case to answer, or upon the receipt of new evidence.

So if you are subject to a complaint check the up to date ARB Investigation Rules as well as any guidance notes published that deal with the practical application of the changed rules.

At the time of going to press, if the IC decides there is a case to answer and refers it to the PCC for a public hearing, the architect has the right to ask the ARB Registrar to consider any overlooked or new evidence and if appropriate to refer the case back to the IC for further consideration.

If the decision not to refer the complaint to the PCC is upheld then the architect or the client may ask for an independent third party review as to whether the ARB has handled the case in accordance with its procedures and guidance. The review conducted by an independent party does not consider the merits of the case or the decision to refer, but only whether the ARB has handled it correctly. If that were to be the decision of the independent reviewer the case is referred back to the IC to review its decision, but it is not obliged to change it.

If the IC does not consider the complaint serious enough to warrant a PCC hearing, but nevertheless has concerns about the conduct of the architect, it can warn the architect concerned as to future conduct.

The ARB Professional Conduct Committee

The PCC comprises architect and lay members and is chaired by a lawyer appointed by the Law Society. Its decisions are final, but are subject to appeal to the High Court in England and Wales and to the Court of Session in Scotland.

The PCC may make a disciplinary order against a guilty architect, which can be:

- a public reprimand
- suspension for not more than two years
- erasure from the ARB register for at least two years
- a fine of up to £2,500.

If you are found guilty of a disciplinary offence and are removed from the register for more than two years, you will have to satisfy the ARB that you are competent to practise before you can be put back onto the register. The ARB publishes a guide setting out how it decides on competence in those circumstances.

If you receive a notification from the ARB of a complaint against you:

- *treat it seriously*, no matter how unfounded or unreasonable you consider it to be
- reply promptly to all correspondence and deal with all accusations objectively and honestly
- seek advice if necessary from an independent experienced architect about the strength of the complaint and how you should answer the technical or architectural issues it raises
- if the matter is serious and is to be the subject of a PCC hearing, take legal advice as to your rights and how best to present your defence.

PCC hearings are held in public, with press present. Case decisions are published and can be widely reported. Avoid discussing the complaint with the media before the hearing. Although the matter is confidential until the public hearing, complainants (and sometimes the architects involved) have been known to seek publicity in advance of the hearing. It may not help your case if details of the complaint appear in the press before the PCC has considered the issues and come to a decision.

Your professional reputation will almost certainly suffer if you get into trouble with the ARB.

Complaints must fall under one of the two disciplinary headings in the Architects Act 1997:

- 'Unacceptable professional conduct' primarily deals with ethical behaviour as a professional. This could include such matters as conflicts of interest, not having the appropriate PII cover, mishandling clients' money, not having a written client agreement and breaching client confidentiality. Each complaint is, however, treated on its own merits.
- 'Serious professional incompetence' covers the competence of architects in their practice of architecture. This is defined in the code as 'a service which falls short of the standards required of a registered person'. To be a punishable disciplinary offence, the PCC must be satisfied that there has been an incompetent act or series of acts which amount to serious professional incompetence.

Clearly, each complaint is treated on its particular circumstances, but in general terms a single incompetent act, unless it had very serious consequences, might warrant no more than a written warning and may not in itself be considered 'serious professional incompetence'. But a series of less serious incompetent acts could, together, be considered sufficient to warrant a charge.

Acts that could lead to a serious incompetence charge would include many of the potential practical tripwires identified in this guide. As most complaints of incompetence usually relate to allegations of increased building cost and time overruns, control of costs and avoidance of delays are crucial if you are to reduce your risk of being the subject of a complaint of serious professional incompetence.

The following is a summary of the ten most common complaints made against architects to the ARB.

These are the tripwires to avoid if you want to avoid a complaint to the ARB (and the RIBA as well)!

1. *Delays in completion*
    Optimistic projections as to how long it will take to complete the project and not warning the clients of delays when they occur.

2. *Unrealistic design in relation to client's budget*
    Raising the client's expectations too high in terms of the budget available, resulting in the project having to be scaled down or abandoned.

3. *Mistakes by the architect*
    Errors in design by the architect, resulting in extra costs to the client.

4. *Ambiguous contracts*
    Complaints about lack of proper contract documentation and proper definition of the architect's responsibilities under the contract.

5. *Advice outside the architect's competence*
    Complaints relating to instances where architects have claimed expertise which it subsequently appears they did not possess.

6. *Communication problems*
    Lack of proper advice or warnings by architects on delays and, particularly, escalating costs.

7. *Post-completion problems*
    Failure to deal properly with defect problems that arise with the building after final completion of the contract.

8. **Bad advice**
    Recommending contractors, materials and other matters sometimes beyond their technical and professional competence.

9. **Conflicts of interest**
    Non-disclosure of on-going business relationships between the architect and contractor and others, leading to suspicion that the architect is not acting in the best interests of the client.

10. **Work carried out by office 'juniors'**
    Work on the client's project delegated to junior staff who did not have the necessary skills to work with minimal supervision. Architects delegating duties that are outside the competence of the staff member.

The ARB publishes a list of PCC decisions in detail back to 2008 and more generally back to 1999. It is worth reading as it sets out many of the tripwires for the unwary architect to avoid if they are to keep out of trouble with the ARB.

The Royal Institute of British Architects

Once you are qualified as an architect you also have the opportunity of joining the RIBA. This enables you to use the affix 'RIBA' after your name and describe yourself as a 'chartered architect' – provided that at the same time you are on the ARB register and so entitled to practise using the title 'architect'. The proportion of UK architects who choose to be members of the RIBA as well as being on the ARB register has varied between 80 per cent and 90 per cent. RIBA members may also belong to the Royal Incorporation of Architects in Scotland (RIAS), the Royal Society of Architects in Wales (RSAW) or the Royal Society of Ulster Architects (RSUA). (The Association of Consultant Architects, the ACA, is a separate association of private-practice architects.)

The RIBA also publishes a code of conduct, which it expects its members to adhere to, and has a disciplinary procedure which can lead to finding a member guilty of a breach of the RIBA code. If you are a member found guilty of a breach you may be reprimanded, and if the breach is sufficiently severe you may be suspended or expelled from RIBA membership. The RIBA code is similar to the ARB's Architects Code, but it includes additional issues relating to professionalism, particularly relationships with others (i.e. fellow architect and other professionals, clients and the public).

The ARB and the RIBA: how does it work in practice?

If you are found guilty of unacceptable professional conduct or serious professional incompetence by the ARB's PCC and are reprimanded, suspended or erased from the register, the RIBA may accept this finding without conducting a separate investigation. You will be offered the opportunity to make a plea in mitigation to demonstrate why you should not similarly be sanctioned by the Institute.

It is important to note that the courts (not the ARB) have decided that if you are not on the ARB register then you cannot use the RIBA affix – this is because the initial 'A' is for 'Architects', which is a title restricted to those on the statutory register.

The *RIBA Code of Professional Conduct*

The *RIBA Code of Professional Conduct* (updated in January 2005) is based on its three principles of professional conduct:

1. **Integrity:** act with honesty and integrity at all times.
2. **Competence:** members must act competently, conscientiously, responsibly and provide the knowledge, ability and financial and technical resources appropriate for their work.
3. **Relationships:** respect the relevant rights and interests of others.

The code offers brief guidance on how each of the principles may be upheld:

Honesty and integrity

1.1   The Royal Institute expects its Members to act with impartiality, responsibility and truthfulness at all times in their professional and business activities.

1.2   Members should not allow themselves to be improperly influenced either by their own, or others', self-interest.

1.3   Members should not be a party to any statement which they know to be untrue, misleading, unfair to others or contrary to their own professional knowledge.

1.4   Members should avoid conflicts of interest. If a conflict arises, they should declare it to those parties affected and either remove its cause, or withdraw from that situation.

1.5   Members should respect confidentiality and the privacy of others.

1.6   Members should not offer or take bribes in connection with their professional work.

Competence

2.1 Members are expected to apply high standards of skill, knowledge and care in all their work. They must also apply their informed and impartial judgment in reaching any decisions, which may require members to balance differing and sometimes opposing demands (for example, the stakeholders' interests with the community's and the project's capital costs with its overall performance).

2.2 Members should realistically appraise their ability to undertake and achieve any proposed work. They should also make their clients aware of the likelihood of achieving the client's requirements and aspirations. If members feel they are unable to comply, they should not quote for, or accept, the work.

2.3 Members should ensure that their terms of appointment, the scope of their work and the essential project requirements are clear and recorded in writing. They should explain to their clients the implications of any conditions of engagement and how their fees are to be calculated and charged. Members should maintain appropriate records throughout their engagement.

2.4 Members should keep their clients informed of the progress of a project and of the key decisions made on the client's behalf.

2.5 Members are expected to use their best endeavours to meet the client's agreed time, cost and quality requirements for the project.

Relationships

3.1 Members should respect the beliefs and opinions of other people, recognise social diversity and treat everyone fairly. They should also have a proper concern and due regard for the effect that their work may have on its users and the local community.

3.2 Members should be aware of the environmental impact of their work.

3.3 Members are expected to comply with good employment practice and the RIBA Employment Policy, in their capacity as an employer or an employee.

3.4 Where members are engaged in any form of competition to win work or awards, they should act fairly and honestly with potential clients and competitors. Any competition process in which they are participating must be known to be reason-able, transparent and impartial. If members find this not to be the case, they should endeavour to rectify the competition process or withdraw.

3.5 Members are expected to have in place (or have access to) effective procedures for dealing promptly and appropriately with disputes or complaints.

More detailed advice for members is set out in a series Guidance Notes, which explain how the principles can be upheld. The nine documents, which can be downloaded from the RIBA's website (www.architecture.com/TheRIBA/AboutUs/Ourstructure/Constitution/CodeOfConduct.aspx), cover the following areas:

Note 1: *Integrity, conflicts of interest, confidentiality and privacy, corruption and bribery.* Similar to the ARB code.

Note 2: *Competition.* Similar to the ARB code but includes a note on European Union competition law and architectural competitions.

Note 3: *Advertising.* Wider guidance than with the ARB code, with an annex covering in some detail the use of practice names and descriptions, identifying practice principals, multi-disciplinary practices and the use of the RIBA crest. It also covers the use of the RIBA affix and the need to be registered with the ARB. If you are setting up or are already in practice and you are a member of the RIBA, you would be wise to check with this RIBA guide to ensure you comply.

Note 4: *Appointments.*

Note 5: *PI Insurance.* You must have the maximum PII cover against liability for negligence or breach of contract claims that you can reasonably afford. Adequate PII cover is required by the ARB for individual architects and the RIBA requires that you hold appropriate insurance cover if you wish to be an RIBA Registered practice and to be considered for nomination by the RIBA for work. The annex to this note covers the main RIBA issues relating to PII.

Note 6: *Continuing Professional Development.* The RIBA requires practising members to undertake CPD for as long as they continue in practice. The note sets out the minimum requirements, which are now subject to random checks. The ARB requirements are similar and are set out in its '*Guidelines for Maintaining Competence*' note. If you are applying for readmission to the register, the ARB may require you to produce evidence of CPD in support of your application.

Note 7: *Relationships.* Similar requirements to the ARB code, but includes in addition advice on supplanting and taking over work from other architects.

Note 8: *Employment and equal opportunities.* This covers a number of areas not specifically referred to in the ARB code, including employment of students. The ARB code specifically excludes repeating obligations from laws on discrimination and employment law, which you are expected to comply with anyway. But, as with the RIBA, alleged breaches could be examined in disciplinary proceedings.

Note 9: *Complaints and dispute resolution.* Similar to the ARB code but also includes information on dispute resolution, which annex GN9 deals with in detail covering mediation, adjudication and arbitration.

If you are convicted of a criminal offence (of any kind) which carries a tariff of 12 months or more, you will automatically be expelled. Where the tariff is less than 12 months, the Hearings Panel will determine an appropriate sanction. An application may be made for readmission when the sentence is spent, and this will be considered by the Assessment Panel.

While it is not necessary to be a member of the RIBA to practise using the title 'architect', if you are a member you will wish to protect that membership, quite apart from the problems (such as bad publicity) that may arise if you are expelled or suspended. So do make sure you do not fall foul of the RIBA's membership rules.

RIBA disciplinary procedures

When a complaint is received by the RIBA the member is contacted notifying them of the complaint and requesting comments. The ARB is contacted to establish whether it has received the same complaint and if so how it is dealing with it.

The member's comments are sent to the complainant. If the complaint is to proceed it is referred to the RIBA Assessment Panel and to the ARB.

The Assessment Panel reviews the evidence and if it considers there is a case to answer, it refers the complaint to the Hearings Panel.

The Hearings Panel considers both written and verbal evidence and decides on the appropriate action. If it upholds the complaint the member is allowed to make a plea of mitigation and the sanction on the member is then decided. This can be a private or a public reprimand, suspension from membership for a period of time or, in very serious cases, expulsion from RIBA membership.

If you forfeit your RIBA membership through professional misconduct, you will lose the right to use all RIBA insignia. You will no longer be a 'chartered' architect, nor entitled to use the affix 'RIBA' after your name.

SUMMARY

Keeping out of trouble with the ARB

- The Architects Registration Board has teeth and can bite! The ARB will discipline you if you are found guilty of unacceptable professional conduct, serious professional incompetence or have a criminal conviction that is relevant to your fitness to practise.
- You can be publicly reprimanded, suspended or have your name erased from the ARB register and fined up to £2,500 if found guilty.
- While the ARB's *Architects Code* sets the standards expected of you in your professional conduct and competence, in practice non-compliance is not an offence in itself. Breaches would, however, almost certainly be used as evidence against you in disciplinary proceedings.
- Treat the ARB code as a good practice guide as much as a code of conduct. In that way you will operate an efficient practice and keep out of trouble with your clients and the ARB.
- Resolve disputes with clients without delay, before they become major problems leading to formal complaints to the ARB.
- On receipt of notification of a complaint from the ARB, treat it seriously, no matter how absurd you consider it to be. Deal with all correspondence with the ARB objectively and without delay.
- Take architectural and, if necessary, legal advice about the validity of a complaint and how you will be represented at the PCC hearing.
- Avoid discussing your case in the press before the hearing. It is unlikely to be helpful.

Keeping out of trouble with the RIBA

- The *RIBA Code of Professional Conduct* sets high standards of behaviour expected of all members. Its series of guidance notes are intended to help you provide a professional and competent service and behave in a professional, responsible and ethical manner.
- The RIBA's disciplinary procedures are conducted in confidence. Breaches of confidentiality may be regarded as breaches of the code.

CONTINUED ▶

SUMMARY (CONTINUED)

- If you are found guilty of breaching the *RIBA Code of Professional Conduct* you can be publicly reprimanded, suspended or expelled from membership.
- If you are suspended or expelled you will lose all membership rights, most particularly the rights to use the RIBA crest and affix.
- The RIBA offers alternative dispute resolution services (mediation, adjudication and arbitration) – use them before a problem deteriorates into a formal complaint about your professional behaviour.
- Co-operate with Institute procedures – don't think that a formal complaint can be ignored.

Bibliography

A guide to letter contracts: for very small projects, surveys and reports, 3rd edn (2012) RIBA Publishing.

Architects Registration Board. *Architects Code: Standards of Conduct and Practice.* ARB. Online at: www.arb.org.uk

Architects Registration Board. *PII Guidelines*. ARB. Online at: www.arb.org.uk

Construction Companion: Briefing (2002) RIBA Publishing.

Royal Institute of British Architects (2005). *RIBA Code of Professional Conduct.* RIBA

Index